COMETS

Patrick Moore is the author of, among other books:

The Amateur Astronomer

New Guide to the Planets

New Guide to the Stars

Can You Speak Venusian?

Black Holes in Space (with Iain Nicolson)

COMETS

PATRICK MOORE

CHARLES SCRIBNER'S SONS
NEW YORK

1 3 5 7 9 11 13 15 17 19 H/C 20 18 16 14 12 10 8 6 4 2
1 3 5 7 9 11 13 15 17 19 M/P 20 18 16 14 12 10 8 6 4 2

Printed in the United States of America
Library of Congress Catalog Card Number 76–24937
ISBN 0–684–14749–1 (cloth)
ISBN 0–684–15581–8 (paper)

CONTENTS

v

LIST OF ILLUSTRATIONS

PREFACE TO THE REVISED EDITION

The first edition of this book appeared in 1973. For the new version I have enlarged and updated the text and have included many new illustrations. I am most grateful to Commander H. R. Hatfield, Jack Bennett, D. G. Daniels, Jack McBain, K. Kennedy, and the late Dr. E. M. Lindsay for allowing me to use their photographs. I wish also to thank the Mount Wilson and Palomar Observatories and the Royal Greenwich Observatory, Herstmonceux.

1 VISITORS FROM SPACE

When beggars die, there are no comets seen;
The heavens themselves blaze forth the death of princes.

(*Julius Caesar*, II, 2)

The words are Shakespeare's; the belief is very old indeed. For many centuries, and indeed until relatively modern times, comets were regarded as messengers of disaster. There were even suggestions that a collision with a comet could bring about the end of the world. Certainly the spectacle of a great comet, with a brilliant head and a tail stretching halfway across the sky, could well be expected to strike terror into the hearts of primitive peoples, but the fear of comets lingered on for a surprisingly long time and is still not entirely dead. On my desk I have a pamphlet entitled *The Christmas Monster* in reference to a comet (Kohoutek's) which was expected to become really bright toward the end of 1973. The pamphlet, put out by a religious sect, made all manner of dire forecasts, including worldwide destruction, and was widely distributed. Ironically, the comet itself proved to be a great disappointment.

Of course, there is no reason whatsoever for anyone to be alarmed by comets. They are harmless, and they are fascinating; by now a great deal has been learned about them, and plans are being made to send up a space probe to rendezvous with a suitable comet. Any such idea would have seemed fantastic only a few decades ago, but there is nothing farfetched about it today.

Comets, like the earth, belong to the solar system, so before explaining their natures, a brief survey of this part of the universe seems in order.

The solar system is made up of one star (the sun), nine principal planets (of which the earth comes third in order of distance), and various bodies of lesser importance. Among the latter are the satellites which attend some of the planets. The earth has one satellite, our familiar moon, which keeps it company in its never-ending journey around the sun. The moon is less than a quarter of a million miles away, so that astronomically speaking it is on the earth's doorstep. Recently I checked the dashboard of my elderly car and found that the miles covered during the past twenty years exceeded 600,000. This means that I have driven more than twice the distance to the moon.

In general, however, the solar system is built on a grand scale. The sun, 93 million miles from the earth, is only an average star—much less luminous than many of the stars visible on any clear night—but it is the center of the system and controls all the other members. The planets themselves move in paths or orbits that are not very different from circles, and they shine by reflecting the light of the sun, so that they appear starlike. Venus, Mars, and Jupiter may outshine even the most brilliant of the stars, while Saturn also is a conspicuous object, and Mercury is not hard to see in the dusk or dawn sky when it is in a favorable position in relation to the sun. The remaining planets (Uranus,

Neptune, and Pluto) are fainter and were discovered only in more modern times: Uranus in 1781, Neptune in 1846, and Pluto as recently as 1930. Pluto, incidentally, has an orbit which is relatively eccentric, and it may not deserve to rank as a true planet at all. There are suggestions that it is merely an ex-satellite of Neptune that managed to break free and move off independently.

The nighttime stars are much more remote than the sun. Even the nearest of them is more than 24 million million miles away, so that its light, moving at 186,000 miles per second, takes 4.2 years to reach us; we say, therefore, that the distance of this particular star (Proxima Centauri) is 4.2 light-years. Most of the rest are more remote still; for example, Rigel in Orion is at a distance of about 900 light-years, so that we see it today as it was in the time of William the Conqueror. This explains both why the stars look so much fainter than the sun and why their individual movements seem very slow. The star patterns, or constellations, appear virtually the same today as they must have to the builders of the Egyptian Pyramids. The planets, which are much closer, wander about from one constellation to another, although admittedly they keep within certain well-defined limits. The word *planet*, which comes from Greek, means "wanderer."

The solar system is divided into two main parts. There are four comparatively small solid planets (Mercury, Venus, Earth, and Mars), with distances from the sun ranging between 36 million and 141 million miles. (These are mean values, suitably rounded off.) Then comes a wide gap in which move thousands of dwarf worlds known as asteroids, or minor planets; even the largest of these, Ceres, is much smaller than the moon, with a diameter of no more than 800 miles at most. Beyond the asteroids come the four giant planets (Jupiter, Saturn, Uranus, and Neptune), with distances ranging from 483 million miles for Jupiter to 2,793 million miles for Neptune. Pluto, which is certainly smaller than Earth, is farther out than Neptune over most of its orbit, but at its nearest to the sun comes closer than Neptune does. However, its orbit is tilted at the relatively sharp angle of 17 degrees, so there is no fear of a collision on the line.

Among the numerous other bodies in the solar system, there are, to begin with, the satellites, or moons: Jupiter has fourteen, Saturn ten, Uranus five, and Neptune and Mars two each, while Earth, of course, has one. Then there are meteors and meteorites, countless particles of varying sizes known collectively as meteoroids, which we can see only when they come so close to the earth that they dash into its atmosphere. Finally, there are those strange, erratic wanderers, the comets.

Many people write to me to say, in various ways, "Last night I saw a bright object flashing across the sky; can it have been a comet?" The answer is quite definitely, "No." Comets lie well beyond the top of the earth's atmosphere and are in orbit around the sun. This means that a comet does not move perceptibly over a few seconds or even a few minutes, and one sometimes has to watch it for hours before detecting any motion against the starry background. An object traveling quickly along, if it is astronomical in nature, must be either a meteor or an artificial satellite.

In 1957 the Russians launched the first orbital vehicle in history, Sputnik 1; since then many hundreds have been sent up, and because they too reflect the sunlight they look like moving stars. A few, such as the balloon Echo satellites of the 1960s, can be very brilliant and have given rise to scores of flying saucer reports. Artificial satellites are outside the scope of a book on comets, but the important thing to remember about these satellites is that if they are put into stable orbits around the earth, far enough out to avoid friction against the upper air, they move in precisely the same way that natural astronomical bodies would. This applies also to the true space stations, of which Skylab of 1973 was the first.

Meteors, however, are relevant because they are closely associated with comets, and this is discussed in Chapter 8. A meteor is a tiny particle, of sand-grain size or less, moving around the sun. If one of these comes close enough to the earth (below 120 miles or so), it has to force its way through the air particles. This sets up friction, heat is generated, and the meteor destroys itself, producing the streak of light which is called a shooting star. When the earth passes through a swarm of meteors, as happens several times in each year, we see a shower of shooting stars. August is a particularly good "meteor month," and anyone who stares upward at a dark, cloudless sky for a few minutes at any time during the first fortnight of August will be very unlucky not to see a meteor or two.

Now and then larger objects drop to ground level without these are then known as mete have meteorite collections, and taria, notably the Hayden Planetarium in New York, which displays a huge meteorite weighing well over 30 tons. It was found by the American arctic explorer Admiral Robert E. Peary in Greenland and remains the largest meteorite "in captivity." The largest known meteorite is still lying where it fell, at Hoba West, near Grootfontein in southern Africa; I doubt that anyone will try to run away with it, since the total weight exceeds 60 tons. Meteorites seem to be basically different in nature from meteors and more closely related to the asteroids.

Comets are different again, and it should be stressed at once that they are not nearly so important as they sometimes look. There have been comets brilliant enough to be seen in broad daylight, but their mass is very small compared with that of a planet, or even a satellite such as the moon. It has been said that a comet is the nearest approach to nothing that can still be anything. We are dealing with a body made up of small, solid particles, ice of various kinds, and extremely thin gas.

A bright comet is composed of three main parts. First there is the nucleus, which contains most of the total mass but is never more than a few miles in diameter (and it is by no means certain that all comets have well-defined nuclei). Around this is the head, or coma, which contains small particles made up of materials such as iron, nickel, and magnesium, together with icy substances in which frozen water, ammonia, and methane are thought to be the most important constituents. In some cases the coma may be huge; that of Great Comet of 1811 had a diameter of 1,250,000 miles, so that it was much bigger than the sun. Extending away from the coma there may be a tail, composed of even smaller particles ("dust") or of incredibly tenuous gas. The Great Comet of 1843 had a tail 200 million miles long, which is greater than the distance between the sun and Mars. On the other hand, many small comets have no tails at all and look like nothing more than small, fuzzy patches in the sky. It has been said that they give the impression of dimly shining cotton wool.

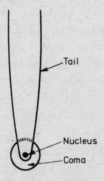

Fig. 1. Physical structure of a comet, showing the nucleus, coma, and tail. Not all comets have visible nuclei, and many of them have no tails.

Left to itself, a comet would not shine at all, but when it nears the sun it is lit up, and we see it by reflection. In the thin stuff of the coma there also occurs the phenomenon known as fluorescence. This means, in effect, that the sunlight is absorbed at one wavelength and re-emitted at another. It is easy to understand, then, why a comet brightens up quickly as it comes sunward and fades equally quickly as it recedes. Moreover, the tail is formed by evaporation of the icy materials and by the driving out of small particles from the nucleus, so that it develops only as the comet moves into the sun's neighborhood.

Some comets have a tail made up of gas, others one of dust; some comets have both. Generally the gas tail is fairly straight and the dust tail noticeably curved, because the dusty particles tend to lag behind as the comet moves onward. Sometimes, of course, the tail is seen from an angle which makes it look shorter than it really is; if, for instance, the comet is heading straight toward us, the tail will not be seen to best advantage. Tail structure can sometimes be very complex, and

Fig. 2. A comet's tail always points more or less away from the sun because of the repelling effect of solar wind, i.e., the low-energy particles being sent out from the sun constantly in all directions. When traveling outward, therefore, the comet moves more or less tail first.

there are rapid, involved changes, with distinct condensations, jets, and streamers. Despite its flimsy nature, a comet is anything but inactive.

One very interesting fact is that a tail always points more or less away from the sun, as shown in Fig. 2, so that during the outward journey the comet actually travels tail first. This has been known for a long time, and various theories have been put forward to account for it. One suggestion, proposed some seventy years ago, involved the pressure of sunlight. Light does exert a pressure, and a light source will tend to push objects away from it, as was proved experimentally in 1900 by the Russian physicist Pyotr Lebedev. By everyday standards the force is very feeble; the repulsive force of sunlight on a square foot of the earth's surface can never be more than 1/10,000,000 of a pound. But in a comet's tail, the particles are very tiny, and radiation pressure has to be balanced against the attractive force of gravitation. It was calculated that for particles about 1/100,000 inch in diameter, radiation pressure would win the tug of war, so that the "dust" in a comet's tail would be driven outward from the nucleus.

Recently there has been a change in outlook, and theorists have tended to look toward what is called "solar wind"—a constant stream of electrified, low-energy particles streaming out from the sun in all directions. Most astronomers now believe that the solar wind exercises the main influence on the direction of a comet's tail, although the full details about what is happening are still not known.

When a brilliant comet with a long tail swings around as it reaches its perihelion (its closest approach to the sun), the tail must presumably sweep around too, but if the tail is millions of miles long, the velocity of its "far end" would have to be improbably high. Therefore, we have to assume that the old tail is largely destroyed and a new one formed fairly quickly. Comets have been known to suffer considerably during their rush past the sun and to have been much fainter after perihelion than before. In any case, there is no doubt that a comet loses some of its material every time it passes perihelion. There is steady wastage, and dusty material is left scattered along the orbit. It follows that, compared with a planet or a satellite, a comet has a very limited life span.

Some comets, at least, are surrounded by huge clouds of the lightest of all gases, hydrogen. These clouds cannot be seen directly, since they radiate only in the ultraviolet range, but are detected by instruments carried in space probes. The first one was discovered in 1968, when a reasonably conspicuous comet, known as Tago–Sato–Kosaka in honor of its three Japanese discoverers, was studied from the space probe OAO2 (Orbiting Astronomical Observatory No. 2) and was found to have a hydrogen cloud a million miles in diameter. Similar clouds were found with Bennett's Comet of 1970 and Kohoutek's Comet of 1973, which was, incidentally, the first comet to be studied from a manned satellite (Skylab). There is no reason to doubt that clouds of the same kind are associated with other comets. All in all, a comet is a much more complicated structure than it might seem.

Obviously, the telescope is astronomers' essential research tool, but they would be lost without the spectroscope, which splits up light and tells what substances exist in the light source itself. Spectroscopy can show which elements are present in the sun, the other stars, the great gas clouds or nebulae, and even in galaxies so far away that their light takes millions of years to reach us. Astronomers have come a long way since 1830, when the French philosopher Auguste Comte predicted that the chemistry of the stars would forever remain a mystery to mankind.

The first attempt to study the spectrum of a comet was made in 1864 by an Italian astronomer, Giovanni Battista Donati. When he turned his spectroscope toward a comet which happened to be on view, he made a fascinating discovery. Since a comet shines essentially by reflected sunlight, Donati expected to see a weak solar spectrum. He did, but he also saw effects which could be due only to light emitted by the gases in the comet on their own account. Donati could take matters little further, since in those days spectroscopy was in its infancy, but by now many different kinds of substances have been identified. Some of the gases are toxic if dense, but since the gas in a comet is many millions of times more rarefied than air, it can do no damage at all. Even a direct collision with the nucleus of a comet would produce only local effects; in fact, there is excellent evidence (discussed in Chapter 8) that a small comet really did hit the earth in 1908.

Various theories about the make-up of comets have been put forward. One of these, due mainly to the British astronomer R. A. Lyttleton, is that of the "flying gravel-bank." According to Lyttleton, both nucleus and coma are made up of dust particles, concentrated toward the center of the comet and making the nucleus appear deceptively solid. As the comet nears the sun and is warmed, the gases inside the dust particles escape, and a tail is formed. Each particle is moving around the sun in its own independent path, but near perihelion the whole structure becomes more crowded; particles collide with one another and are pulverized, producing even more finely divided material, which is driven out by the pressure of the sun's radiation and the solar wind.

Recent research has cast serious doubt upon the gravel-bank theory, and most astronomers have more faith in the "dirty ice ball" idea developed by the American astronomer Fred L. Whipple. Rather than being made up of a swarm of individual particles, the nucleus—which contains most of the mass of a comet—is composed of what is called a conglomerate. The word comes from the Latin *conglomerare,* to form into a ball; it is used by geologists to describe pieces of fragmented rock held together in finer-grained material. In the Whipple model, a comet's nucleus is a conglomerate of rocky fragments together with "ices"—frozen methane, ammonia, carbon dioxide, and other substances, including water. When the comet approaches perihelion, the ices begin to evaporate. Methane is the first to do so; the others follow, and this at least explains the rapid, irregular changes, notably the pronounced jets which sometimes issue from the nucleus. Confirmation was provided by Kohoutek's Comet, which was found in 1974 to contain large quantities of the ionized water molecule, known to chemists as H_2O+; this identification of water in a comet obviously supports the dirty ice ball theory rather than the flying gravel-bank theory.

Whichever picture is right—or even if both are wrong—comets are unlike any other bodies in the solar system. We do not yet understand them fully, but when a space probe can be sent through one of these eerie visitors, many of the outstanding problems should be solved.

2 COMET LORE

Because comets can be so spectacular, records of them go back for many centuries. The same is true of total eclipses of the sun, when for a few minutes "day is turned into night" as the moon covers up the brilliant solar disk. It is not surprising that, before true science began, such events created considerable alarm.

To the Chinese, eclipses were caused by a hungry dragon which was trying to gobble up the sun and had to be scared away by banging gongs and drums and making as much noise as possible. Since an eclipse is of brief duration, the procedure always worked. A comet, on the other hand, can loom balefully in the sky for days, weeks, or occasionally months. (Comets have not had lengthy viewing times during the twentieth century. However, in the nineteenth century there were several really impressive comets, especially those of 1811, 1843, 1858, 1861, and 1882.) Until the sixteenth century, comets were generally regarded as signs of divine displeasure, and there were no obvious ways of pacifying the gods; no amount of gong beating would make a comet go away. Even the Greeks had no idea of their true nature. Anaxagoras (c. 500–426 B.C.) had remarkable insight and believed the sun to be a red-hot stone larger than the Peloponnesus, the peninsula upon which Athens stands, but he thought that comets were produced by the clustering of faint stars. Around 350

B.C. Aristotle taught that both comets and meteors were due to "hot, dry exhalations" rising from the ground and being carried along by the motion of the sky, thus becoming heated and bursting into flame; slow movement produced a comet, rapid movement a meteor. Aristotle's authority was so great that for many centuries after his death the idea of comets as upper-air phenomena was generally accepted.

The Roman scholar Pliny the Elder (A.D. 22–79) commented:

We have, in the war between Caesar and Pompey, an example of the terrible effects which follow the apparition of a comet. Toward the commencement of this war, the darkest nights were made light, according to Lucan, by unknown stars; the heavens appeared on fire; burning torches traversed in all directions the depths of space; the comet, that fearful star, which overthrows the powers of the Earth, showed its terrible locks.

Vespasian, one of the better emperors, refused to be alarmed by the comet of A.D. 79 and is said to have remarked: "This hairy star does not concern me; it menaces rather the King of the Parthians, for he is hairy while I am bald." Despite this confidence, Vespasian died in the same year. Another emperor to die during the visibility of a bright comet was Macrinus, in A.D. 218. However, Macrinus was no Vespasian; he was merely one of the succession of nonentities who occupied the throne during the period following the death of the philosopher-emperor Marcus Aurelius. (In fact, the comet of 218 was Halley's, which is discussed in detail in Chapter 6. It was also on view in 1066, when the Normans were preparing to invade England, and in 1456, when Pope Calixtus III was later said to have excommunicated it.)

The first real advance in cometary studies was made in 1577 by the Danish astronomer Tycho Brahe. Tycho was an extraordinary man; he was much the greatest observer of pre-telescopic times, and for twenty years he worked away on his island observatory at Hven, in the Baltic, drawing up an accurate star catalogue and measuring the apparent movements of the planets. It was his work which enabled his last assistant, Johannes Kepler (1571–1630), to prove that the earth goes around the sun instead of vice versa—something Tycho could never bring himself to believe. While at Hven, Tycho observed seven comets. That of 1577 was fairly bright, and Tycho set out to discover whether it showed any measurable "diurnal parallax." If it were closer than the moon (whose distance was by then known with fair accuracy), it ought to shift against the starry background as the earth turned on its axis; but it did not, and Tycho calculated that the comet must be at least six times as far away as the moon. As we now know, it was considerably more remote than that, but Tycho's reasoning was sound.

The sequel was rather strange. In 1618 an Italian named Orazio Grassi published a book in which he repeated Tycho's conclusions, and he was bitterly attacked by no less a person than Galileo, who was the first great observer to use a telescope and who played a major role in destroying the theory that the sun goes around the earth. The story of how Galileo was subsequently-brought up before the Inquisition and forced into a public and absolutely hollow recantation is too well known to repeat here; but even though he was right about the movement of the earth, he was quite wrong about comets, which he thought to be due to the refraction of sunlight in vapors rising from the earth. In that case, of course, a comet would not show parallax any more than a rainbow does. It is curious that a man of Galileo's intelligence should have fallen into such a trap, but he never changed his opinion.

Despite Galileo, the idea of comets as celestial objects was taking hold, even though their nature was still obscure. René Descartes, the seventeenth-century French philosopher who worked out a "theory of vortices" for the universe, supposed comets to be stars which gradually became covered with spots until they lost their light, after which they could not keep their set places in the sky and were carried along until they approached the sun closely enough to be lighted up and made visible. The real change in outlook came with Edmond Halley, who calculated that one particular comet appeared every 76 years or so, traveling in an elliptical path which brought it back regularly to the neighborhood of the sun, and was therefore a bona-fide member of the solar system. The first predicted return of Halley's Comet, in 1758–59, ushered in what we may call the modern era.

The fear of comets was both superstitious and practical. That rather elusive Englishman, Thomas Digges, wrote in 1556: "Comets signify corruption of the stars. They are signs of earthquakes, of wars, of changing of kingdoms, great dearth of corn, yea a

n death of man and beast." (I have modern-
___ spelling.) A remarkable proclamation was is-
sued by the town council at Baden, in Switzerland,
when a comet with "a frightful long tail" appeared
in the year 1681. The town authorities ordered that
"all are to attend Mass and Sermon every Sunday
and Feast Day, not leaving the church before the
sermon or staying away without good reason; all
must abstain from playing or dancing, whether at
weddings or on other occasions; none must wear un-
seemly clothing, nor swear nor curse." Whether
these orders were obeyed to the letter we do not
know. If so, that particular period must have been
rather dull for the Badenese. So far as I have been
able to discover, the last pronouncement of this kind
by a serious astronomer was made on July 4, 1816,
by a certain Dr. Pennada, addressing the Institute of
Padua in Italy. Pennada claimed that "the most remarkable political events have always been pre-
ceded, accompanied or followed by extraordinary
astro-meteorological phenomena"—a clear reference
to comets.

It would be wrong to say that comets have exerted a
great influence upon human thought. They have not;
the ideas about them were merely a part of the general
belief that human destiny was ruled, and even forecast,
by events in the sky. But quite apart from these un-
directed fears there was alarm about the possible
effects of a cometary collision with the earth, and there
have been occasional panics on this score.

Probably the most famous prediction of this kind was
made by the English scholar and clergyman Dr. Wil-

liam Whiston, who was contemporary with Sir Isaac Newton and succeeded him as Lucasian Professor of Mathematics at the University of Cambridge in 1710. Fourteen years earlier Whiston had published his book, *A New Theory of the Earth,* in which he tried to link the Book of Genesis with the wanderings of a comet. Indeed, he believed that the earth itself had begun its career as a comet which periodically approached the sun and was violently heated. As the orbit became more circular, the overheating stopped, and the comet became a planet. Man appeared, but the grievous sins of humanity caused another comet to strike the earth, giving it a movement of rotation and producing a huge tide, which was, of course, the biblical flood. Whiston gave the date of this disaster as either November 28, 2349 B.C., or December 2, 2926 B.C. He predicted that this comet would eventually return, changing the earth's path again and transforming the world once more into a comet, with the inevitable destruction of all life.

Whiston's subsequent career was decidedly checkered; he eventually lost his post as Lucasian Professor because of heretical opinions, but his scientific reputation made some people take his theories seriously. They are, of course, quite absurd. The difference in mass between a comet and even a small planet is tremendous, quite apart from the fact that the bodies are basically different in nature, and there is not the slightest chance of a comet's changing into a planet or vice versa. Yet even in our own time there has been a revival of the idea. In the 1950s several books appeared from the pen of a psychiatrist, Dr. Immanuel Velikovsky, who was born in Russia but has spent most of his life in America. Velikovsky's first offering, entitled *Worlds in Collision,* also confused planets with comets. Other books followed, and a curious cult developed, which still exists.

To Velikovsky, the time scale of the universe is measured in thousands of years rather than in millions. He explains how the giant planet Jupiter suffered a tremendous outburst and shot out a comet which later became the planet Venus. The comet Venus bypassed the earth in 2500 B.C., at the time of the Israelite exodus led by Moses, and slowed down the earth's rotation, drying up the Red Sea at a convenient moment for the Israelites to cross. Tremendous upheavals followed; petrol rained down, so that our modern fuel represents "remnants of the intruding star which poured forth fire and sticky vapour." Two months later, after the earth had started spinning again, the comet Venus returned for a second visit, producing the thunder and lightning noted when Moses received the commandments on Mount Sinai. Other encounters followed, one of which caused the tremors that shook down the walls of Jericho. Then the comet collided with Mars and lost its tail, thus turning into the modern planet Venus. Meanwhile Mars itself moved closer to the earth and almost hit it in 687 B.C. Velikovsky gives instance after instance, all "supported" by quotations from the Bible which are, incidentally, quite accurate.

Nobody with even the most elementary knowledge of science can take this rigmarole seriously, but Velikovsky's theories are at least harmless, and the world would be poorer without its never-ending supply of what I have termed "independent thinkers." (Velikovsky's theories and others of their kind are discussed in my book, *Can You Speak Venusian?*, published in 1972 by W. W. Norton, New York.)

To go back two centuries, there was a panic in France in 1773, which arose from a misinterpretation of a scientific paper written by the eminent mathematician Joseph Jérôme de Lalande. People jumped to the conclusion that a comet would collide with the earth on May 20 or 21 of that year and there were numerous sales of seats in Paradise, which the clergy were said to have obtained by special dispensation. In 1832 there was yet another alarm in France, this time connected with Biela's periodic comet. Calculations showed that the comet would cross the earth's orbit on October 29, but as the world itself was nowhere near that point in its path, there was no cause for apprehension. The distance between the earth and the comet was always well over 40 million miles.

End-of-the-world scares still occur in backward countries. On June 30, 1973, there was a total eclipse of the sun visible from parts of Africa, and a team of European scientists arriving in Kenya were met with hostility from the local inhabitants, who believed that the white men were trying to kill the sun. A comet may not be so startling as a total eclipse, but it certainly lasts far longer, and no doubt the witch doctors will have their say the next time a brilliant comet appears. Bennett's Comet of 1970 caused considerable alarm in Arab countries because it was commonly mistaken for an Israeli war weapon.

It may also be worth recalling that in 1910, when

Halley's Comet was last on view, an enterprising American manufacturer made a large sum of money by selling what he called comet pills, although I have no idea what they were meant to do. Human nature is slow to change.

3 THE PATHS OF COMETS

The belief that comets were luminous effects in the earth's upper atmosphere lasted until 1577, when Tycho showed that the comet of that year lay well beyond the moon. But not until the time of Newton and Halley, in the late seventeenth century, did anyone have a real idea of how a comet moves, and at that time it had only recently been realized that the sun, rather than the earth, lies at the center of the solar system.

According to ancient theories, all celestial orbits were circular, because the circle is the "perfect" form, and nothing short of absolute perfection can be allowed in the heavens. The man who overthrew this concept was Kepler, whose laws of planetary motion were published between 1609 and 1618.

Kepler's first law states that a planet moves around the sun in an ellipse, not a circle. A typical ellipse of low eccentricity is shown in section *a* of Fig. 3. The two points lettered F and F' are the "foci" of the ellipse and are reasonably close together so that the ellipse is not very different from a circle. With a planetary orbit, the sun lies in one focus of the ellipse, while the other focus is empty. The ratio of the distance between the foci to the whole length of the ellipse is a measure of the eccentricity (see Fig. 3). If the foci coincide, the eccentricity is zero, and the result is a circle. In other words, a circle is simply an ellipse with no eccentricity at all. If the distance between the foci is one-third the whole length of the ellipse (AB in section *b*), the eccentricity will be 0.33. If the eccentricity is still greater—say about 0.6—the ellipse will be long and narrow (section *c*).

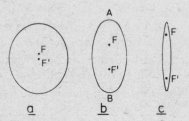

Fig. 3. (a) An ellipse of low eccentricity. F and F' indicate the two foci. (b) An ellipse of higher eccentricity, such as the orbit of a typical short-period comet. (c) An ellipse of high eccentricity, such as the orbit of a comet of a longer period.

The orbits of all the principal planets are of low eccentricity; for instance, the earth's distance from the sun ranges between 91.5 million miles at perihelion to 94.5 million miles at aphelion (greatest recession). Not so with the comets, most of which have paths that are much more elliptical. Finlay's Comet, which has a period of 7 years, has its perihelion at a distance only slightly greater than Earth's but at aphelion moves out well beyond Jupiter. Halley's, with its period of 76 years, recedes beyond Neptune, the outermost of the giant planets.

Some planetary and cometary orbits are shown to scale in Fig. 4. The orbits of the planets from Earth to Neptune are represented; Venus and Mercury, closer in than Earth, cannot be conveniently shown on this scale; Pluto, as was noted, is the "odd man out" and can be disregarded here. Also shown are the orbits of Finlay's Comet and Halley's Comet, as well as part of the orbit of Kohoutek's Comet of 1973. Since both Finlay's and Halley's comets are periodic, we always know when and where to expect them, even though we can see them only when they are moving in the inner part of the solar system. (Farther out, they are too faint to be seen.) But what about Kohoutek's?

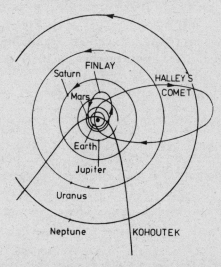

Fig. 4. Orbits of the planets (to scale) and the orbits of Finlay's Comet (short period), Halley's Comet (longer period), and Kohoutek's Comet (nonperiodic).

Here we have a path of a different type. The eccentricity is very great, and so at aphelion the comet will recede to a tremendous distance. Moreover, in the far part of its orbit it moves very slowly, and the result is that it will not come back to perihelion for over 70,000 years. To all intents and purposes, it is a nonperiodic comet. We could not predict it, and this is true of all other bright naked-eye comets with the single exception of Halley's. Our most brilliant visitors arrive unannounced and are apt to take us by surprise.

In an extreme case, a comet may move in an open curve—a path of the kind known as a parabola (See Fig. 5). Obviously, a comet moving in a parabolic path will never come back to the sun at all but will continue moving outward indefinitely. There are also curves which are still more open and are called hyperbolic, but they are of interest only to those who wish to delve deeply into theory.

It used to be thought that some comets come from

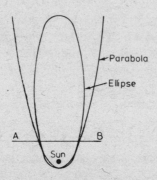

Fig. 5. An ellipse and a parabola. The ellipse is a closed curve, while the parabola is open. When only a portion of the orbit of a comet can be observed (below the line AB in the diagram) it is very difficult to tell whether the comet is moving in a very eccentric ellipse or in a parabola.

interstellar space and pay only one visit to the sun. This view is now not generally held: comets are regarded as genuine members of the solar system. If the orbit becomes "open," the cause is to be found in what are called planetary perturbations.

Remember, a comet is a very flimsy thing and is at the mercy of the gravitational pulls of the planets. If a comet approaches a planet too closely, its orbit will be violently twisted. This has been seen to happen on a number of occasions. Jupiter, by far the most massive of the planets, is particularly powerful as a "comet disturber," and astronomers believe that in an extreme case the comet may be thrown out of the solar system altogether.

Comets, then, may be divided into several classes, depending on their orbits.

Short-period comets. These have periods of between 3.3 years (Encke's Comet) and around 20 years. Many of them have their aphelia at about the mean distance of Jupiter, which again demonstrates how influential that planet is. When these comets are very distant, they are too dim to be seen, but their paths can be worked out, so we can keep track of them. Encke's Comet, for instance, has now been seen at more than fifty different returns since its original discovery in 1786, and it remains on view for several months during each revolution. Unfortunately, all the short-period comets are faint objects, and most of them are devoid of tails.

Medium-period comets. These have orbits that are generally larger and more eccentric. Crommelin's

Comet has a period of 28 years, and its distance ranges
between that of Venus and that of Uranus. However,
occasional comets in this category have much more
circular paths; the orbit of Comet Schwassmann–Wachmann 1, for instance, lies wholly between that of Jupiter and that of Saturn, so that it is never out of view
because of distance.

Long-period comets. These have periods of from about
60 years to as much as 164 years. Comet Grigg–Mellish,
which has the longest period of any comet to have been
seen at more than one return, can come within the
orbit of Earth, but at aphelion it recedes to almost twice
the distance of Neptune. So far, seven long-period comets have been seen at only one return, five at more than
one, including Halley's which, with twenty-seven returns, holds the record.

Nonperiodic comets. These comets move in a parabola,
a hyperbola, or a very eccentric ellipse. This class includes all the really brilliant comets as well as many
fainter ones. Strictly speaking, the term is misleading,
because at least some of the so-called nonperiodic comets move in elliptical paths. Yet because they come to
perihelion only once in many centuries (or, sometimes,
once in millions of years), they cannot be predicted.
Obviously it is difficult to tell whether a comet of this
kind is moving in an eccentric ellipse or in an open
curve (a parabola or hyperbola), and any calculations
are necessarily arbitrary. Kohoutek's Comet of 1973 is
estimated to have a period of about 75,000 years. That
of Delavan's Comet of 1914 was calculated to be 24

million years, but all we can really say is that it will not be seen again for an extremely long time, if at all. The last reasonably bright comet, West's Comet of 1976, is also moving in an orbit which will not bring it back to the inner part of the solar system for many centuries.

Clearly, then, most cometary orbits are very different from those of the planets so far as eccentricity is concerned. Moreover, the planets have paths which are more or less in the same plane. Except for Pluto, the inclinations are less than 8 degrees with respect to the orbit of Earth, so that a plan of the solar system drawn

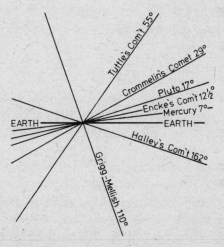

Fig. 6. Inclinations of the orbits of some comets and planets, in relation to the plane of the earth's orbit. The inclinations are less than 4 degrees for all the planets except for Mercury and Pluto. Comets may have orbits of very high inclination. Of those shown in the diagram, Halley and Grigg–Mellish move in a retrograde direction.

on a flat piece of paper is not very inaccurate. With comets, the inclinations may be of any value—29 degrees for Crommelin's Comet, 12.5 degrees for Encke's, and so on, as shown in Fig. 6. There are also various comets which travel in a retrograde (opposite) direction as compared with the planets, rather in the manner of cars going the wrong way around a traffic island. Halley's Comet belongs to the retrograde class.

Having discussed Kepler's first law (a planet moves in an elliptical orbit, with the sun as one focus of the ellipse), let us turn to his second law, which states that a line drawn from a planet to the sun will sweep over equal areas in equal times. This means that a body moving around the sun will travel quickest when it is closest in, more slowly when it moves farther out. Thus, in Fig. 7, representing the orbit of a comet, the time taken for the comet to move from A to B will be the same as the time taken for it to move from C to D. With S representing the sun, the shaded area ASB must be equal to the shaded area CSD. Consequently, a comet will spend most of its time in the remoter part of its orbit and will move very quickly as it passes through perihelion.

Because a comet is so much influenced by the planets, it will never follow exactly the same path at successive returns, and in some cases the orbit may be violently disturbed. A classic case is that of Lexell's Comet of 1770, which came within 1.5 million miles of the earth and was visible with the naked eye. Its period was then calculated to be about 5.5 years, but it has never been seen again, because it subsequently made a close approach to Jupiter, and in its new orbit, it stays so far

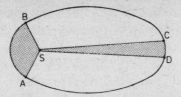

Fig. 7. Kepler's second law. The object moves most quickly when it is nearest to the sun, so it moves from A to B in the same time that it takes to move from C to D. The area ASB is equal to the area CSD.

away from Earth that nobody has been able to track it down. A naked-eye comet discovered by the Italian astronomer Francesco di Vico in 1844 (and rediscovered in 1894 by the American astronomer Lewis Swift and hence named Di Vico–Swift) has suffered several series of perturbations by Jupiter and at present does not come close enough to Earth to be visible without a telescope. Between 1894 and 1965 it "went missing," and its recovery in the latter year was very much of a mathematical triumph.

Astronomers often speak of Jupiter's "comet family," since, as noted, many short-period comets have their aphelia at approximately the distance of Jupiter from the sun (rather less than 500 million miles on the average). Originally it was thought that comets came from outer space and were literally captured by Jupiter, so that they were forced to remain as members of the inner solar system. This intriguing idea has long since been consigned to the scientific scrap heap, and it is not certain whether any planet, even Jupiter, is capable of permanently expelling a comet from the solar system, although the influence of the giant planet is obvious enough. I suggest that alleged comet families associated with the other giants (Saturn, Uranus, and Neptune) must be regarded as highly dubious.

To calculate a comet's orbit is no easy task, although nowadays a great deal of useful work in this direction is carried out by talented amateur mathematicians. Before the first predicted return of Halley's Comet in 1758–59, all comets had been regarded as cosmic strays. Even Kepler believed that they traveled in straight lines through space rather than obeyed the laws he had drawn up for planets.

Comet nomenclature is rather complicated. In most cases a comet is named in honor of its discoverer; D'Arrest's periodic comet was first seen in 1851 by the German astronomer Heinrich Louis D'Arrest. If the same discoverer has more than one comet to his credit, a number is added after his name to show the sequence —Brooks 1, Brooks 2, and so on. Where two or more astronomers are concerned in a discovery, their names are hyphenated; this explains Schwassmann–Wachmann, Grigg–Mellish, Giacobini–Zinner, Arend–Roland, Tuttle–Giacobini–Kresák, and many others. Sometimes the name commemorates the mathematician who first computed the orbit; such are the comets of Encke, Lexell, Crommelin, and Halley.

When a comet is first seen, it is labeled by the year and a letter; thus the first comet to be discovered in 1975 became 1975a, the second 1975b, and so on. A more permanent designation follows the date of perihelion, so that the first comet to reach perihelion in 1975 became 1975 I and the second 1975 II. A year seldom passes without several new comet discoveries.

AN
ALLARM
TO
EUROPE:
By a Late Prodigious
COMET

ſeen *November* and *December*, 1680.

With a Predictive Diſcourſe. Together with ſome preceding and ſome ſucceeding Cauſes of its ſad Effects to the *Eaſt* and *North Eaſtern* parts of the World.

Namely, *ENGLAND*, *SCOTLAND*, *IRELAND*, *FRANCE*, *SPAIN*, *HOLLAND*, *GERMANT*, *ITALT*, and many other places.

By *John Hill* Phyſitian and Aſtrologer.

The Form of the *COMET* with its Blaze or Stream as it was ſeen *December* the 24th. Anno 1680. In the Evening.

London Printed by *H. Brugis* for *William Thackry* at the Angel in Duck-Lane.

Title page of *An Allarm to Europe,* written in 1680 by John Hill.

The Andromeda Galaxy (M31), in the center, looks very much like a comet on this small scale. Photograph by Commander H. R. Hatfield.

Encke's Comet, November 30, 1828. Drawing by W. Struve.

Comet Brooks 2, photographed from Helwan Observatory with a 30-inch reflector, October 25, 1911.

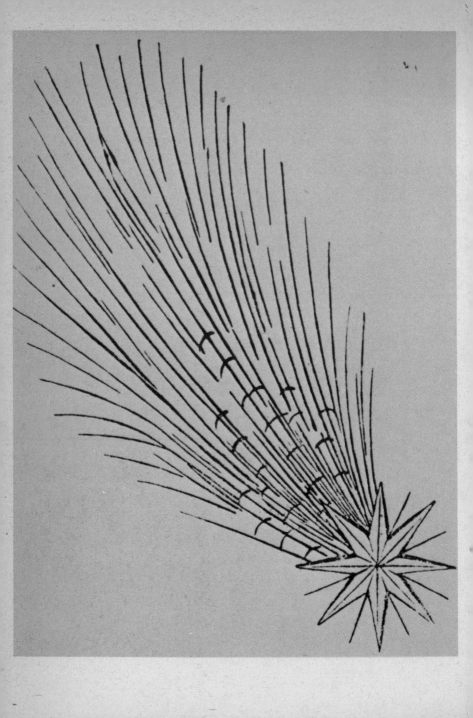

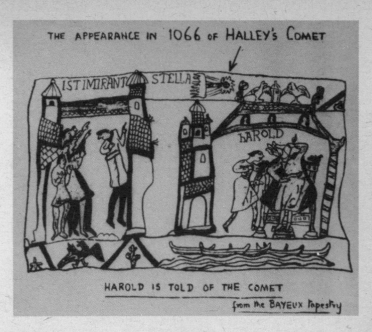

THE APPEARANCE IN 1066 OF HALLEY'S COMET

ISTIMIRANT STELLA

HAROLD

HAROLD IS TOLD OF THE COMET

from the BAYEUX Tapestry

Halley's Comet of 1066 as shown in the Bayeux Tapestry (detail at right). King Harold is alarmed and totters on his throne.

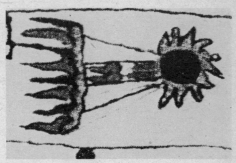

OPPOSITE: Halley's Comet of A.D. 684 as drawn in the *Nürnberg Chronicle*.

Halley's Comet, October 11, 1835. Drawing by C. Piazzi Smyth.

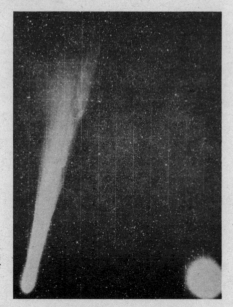

Venus (right) and Halley's Comet, from the Cape of Good Hope, 1910. Photograph by Wood.

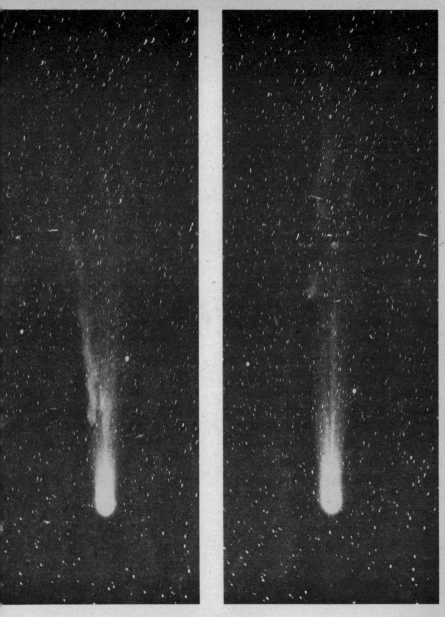

Halley's Comet, from the Lick Observatory, June 6 and 7, 1910. Note the changes in the tail between the two photographs.

De Chéseaux's Comet of 1744 as seen from Lausanne, March 8, 1744.

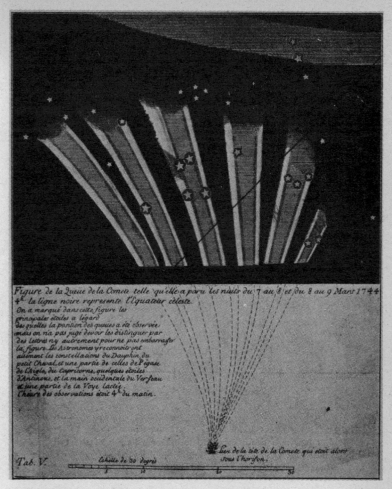

De Chéseaux's drawing of the comet, March 7, 1744.

The Great Comet of 1843. From an old wood-cut.

The Great Comet of 1811. From an old wood-cut.

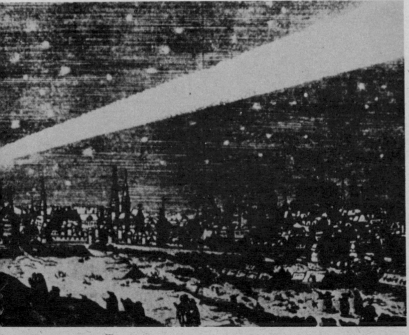

A drawing of the Great Comet of 1843 made by an observer at the Cape of Good Hope. According to many observers, this was the most brilliant comet of the last century.

4 COMET HUNTERS

Modern astronomy has become highly specialized, not only in the professional field, but also among amateurs. Some enthusiastic observers concentrate on studying the sun; others (such as myself) are interested mainly in the moon and the planets; still others are concerned chiefly with variable stars. Comet hunters, generally speaking, are a race apart. They do not need really powerful telescopes; what they must have is a wide field of view and only moderate magnification. Powerful, well-mounted binoculars are ideal, always provided that the observer has a really encyclopedic knowledge of the sky.

The periodic comets—usually very faint—are almost always recovered by professional workers, and there are some specialists, such as Elizabeth Roemer in the United States, who are pre-eminent in this research. But the nonperiodic comets can appear in any part of the sky at any time, and few professionals feel inclined to spend hour after hour scanning the heavens in the hope of picking up a dim new visitor. This is why the amateurs' work is so valuable. Now and then there is what may be called an accidental discovery. A friend of mine once discovered a comet when he was testing a boy's homemade spectacle-lens telescope; he pointed the instrument out of the bedroom window, focused it, and, lo and behold, saw an unknown comet. But in the ordinary way, comet discoveries are made as a result of protracted and painstaking searches.

Looking back over astronomical history, we find some great names in the story of comets, and none is more honored than that of Frenchman Charles-Joseph Messier (1730–1817), even though he is now best remembered for something quite different. He was born in Lorraine and spent most of his active life at the Paris Observatory. His main interest was hunting comets, and altogether he discovered more than a dozen, but for some time he found that he was being plagued by objects which did not interest him in the least. These were star clusters and nebulae.

A comet, as noted, often appears in the guise of a faint luminous patch against the background of stars. The same is true of star clusters, which are exactly what their name implies—groups of associated stars. Some clusters are easy naked-eye objects, and there can be few amateurs who do not know the Pleiades (or Seven Sisters) in the constellation of Taurus, which are prominent in the evening sky for much of the winter and spring. Other naked-eye clusters are the Hyades, also in Taurus, around the bright orange-red star Aldebaran; Praesepe, the Beehive, in Cancer, the Crab; and, in the southern hemisphere, the glorious Jewel Box, Kappa Crucis, in the Southern Cross. Individual stars are very obvious in groups such as these. With fainter, telescopic clusters the separate stars are not as easy to make out, and it is only too easy to confuse a cluster with a comet.

Even greater confusion is caused by nebulae and galaxies. A nebula is a mass of dust and gas, shining because of stars in or close by it; a galaxy is a separate star system, perhaps many millions of light-years away and well outside the Milky Way galaxy which contains the solar system.

As he searched the sky, Messier continually picked up clusters and nebulae. Eventually he lost patience with them. To check each misty object wasted an enormous amount of time; what he needed was a catalogue to which he could refer. Since no such catalogue existed, Messier decided to compile one. In 1781 he published a list of over one hundred clusters, nebulae, and galaxies, giving a number to each object; thus the celebrated Crab Nebula in Taurus became Messier 1 (M1), the Orion Nebula M42, the Andromeda Nebula M31, the Pleiades M45, and so on.

Certainly this made Messier's searches much easier, but the sequel was ironic. Although Messier discovered many comets, it so happened that none of them proved to be particularly bright or particularly interesting, so that they are remembered today only by a relative handful of enthusiasts. On the other hand, his catalogue of clusters and nebulae became a classic, and the M numbers are still used by astronomers all over the world.

Messier continued his comet hunts until late in his life. He had equally enthusiastic contemporaries, such as Pierre Méchain, also of the Paris Observatory, who discovered eight comets between 1781 and 1799. Another was Caroline Herschel (1750–1848), the first and perhaps the most celebrated of all women astronomers. She was the sister of William Herschel, discoverer of the planet Uranus and one of the greatest observers of all time. Herschel undertook systematic "reviews of the heavens" with telescopes he had made himself, and Caroline was his faithful assistant. Night after night she would stay with him, checking and recording as he carried out his work. Not content with this, she conducted comet hunts on her own account and made eight independent discoveries.

Perhaps the strangest career was that of another indefatigable comet hunter of the same period, Jean Louis Pons. In 1789, at the age of twenty-eight, he was appointed to a post at the Marseilles Observatory—as doorkeeper and general handyman! Successive directors took an interest in him, and Pons began to hunt for new comets. Altogether he discovered thirty-seven, which was an amazing feat by any standard. Needless to say, he did not remain a doorkeeper; he rose to the rank of director, first at the Marlia Observatory at Lucca and then at the observatory of Florence.

Three notable American comet hunters of the late nineteenth century were William Brooks, Lewis Swift, and above all Edward Emerson Barnard, who was renowned for his keen eyesight. In his early twenties, in 1881, Barnard discovered a comet which subsequently became brilliant, and he continued to search during most of the rest of his long career, although his most valuable work was in the field of stellar astronomy. Outstanding comet hunters today include Leslie Peltier in the United States, Charles Bradfield in Australia, George Alcock in England, and Jack Bennett in South Africa, to say nothing of the enthusiastic team of searchers in Japan. Alcock, a schoolmaster in Peterborough, now has four comet discoveries to his credit, two of them made within one week. He has also detected

three novae, or new stars. (The name is misleading: a
nova is not a new star, but a formerly faint star which
suffers a violent outburst and flares up to many times its
normal brilliance before fading back to its former ob-
scurity.) Alcock's first nova discovery was made in 1967,
when he detected a particularly interesting object in
the constellation of the Dolphin; it is now known as HR
Delphini. It remained visible to the naked eye for almost a year, and in 1975 it was still within the reach of
comparatively small telescopes.

Alcock does not have a telescope; he uses a pair of
powerful, firmly mounted binoculars. Bennett, who
lives just outside Pretoria, observes with a portable,
wide-field telescope which was originally designed for
following artificial satellites. So far he has found two
comets, plus several others which had been independently detected slightly earlier without his knowledge
and several more which were not confirmed and so are
recorded as "comets that got away." Bennett's first
comet was that of 1970, which was one of the brightest
of modern times. The second was much fainter and
failed to come up to expectations—hardly the fault of
its discoverer. Bennett is also the only living astronomer to have made a visual discovery of a supernova,
which is a titanic stellar outburst in a faraway galaxy. At
the time, Bennett was looking for comets, but as soon
as the galaxy came into the field of his telescope, he
realized that, in his own words, "there was something
wrong with it."

How does one set about searching for comets? Hap-
hazard "sweeping" is of no use at all; the chances
against success are enormous. One must select an area

of the sky and use optical equipment to scan to and fro, noting the familiar stars and checking to see whether anything unusual has made its appearance. I have said that a comet hunter's knowledge of the sky needs to be encyclopedic. Alcock, for example, spent years memorizing the positions and characteristics of some 30,000 stars, so it is not surprising that newcomers will rarely escape him. Few people can achieve such mastery. I have carried out a good deal of lunar and planetary observation, but I am by no means competent to search for comets, as I know very well.

Even when a faint comet is found, it is not always easy to identify. Here I can cite a personal case. Some years ago I was at the Observatory of Armagh, in Northern Ireland, which is equipped with a 10-inch refractor (that is to say, a telescope with its main lens 10 inches in diameter). We had a report that a faint comet had been found, and we were officially asked to confirm it, so I went out to check. I turned the telescope to the indicated position, using the widest field that I could manage, and found nothing. Evidently the position we had been given was wrong, but presumably it could not be greatly in error, so I began searching. Again the result was negative, and I was beginning to lose all confidence when I suddenly observed a very dim patch of light. It could have been a cluster or a nebula, but, unlike Messier, I had adequate catalogues, and a quick search failed to reveal any nebulous object in that area. Probably, then, the faint glow was the comet, but the only way to find out was to watch it until I could detect some movement. After half an hour I was satisfied. The patch had shifted, slowly but perceptibly, against the background stars, and I felt justified in sending off a telegram of confirmation. Undoubtedly it was the comet, but I am sure I would never have noticed it had I not been given all the relevant information. I have tried independent comet hunting as such only twice, both times with negative results.

Today it seldom happens that a comet is not detected before it becomes bright. Most of the major comets are found when they are still a long way from the sun and the earth, although some pass through perihelion without being noticed. Such was Van den Bergh's Comet of 1974, which had the greatest perihelion distance on record—about 560 million miles, so that it never came within the orbit of Jupiter. Although large by cometary standards, it never became bright. The Netherlands-born Canadian astronomer Sidney van den Bergh discovered it, and when the orbit was worked out, it was found that perihelion had been passed previously, on August 14, 1974. The most distant comet ever observed was followed out to a distance of over 1,000 million miles, so that it was then between the orbits of Saturn and Uranus. This was Stearns' Comet of 1927, which was under observation for over four years; had it had a more normal orbit it would have been brilliant, but its minimum distance from the sun was well over 300 million miles.

Once a comet has been found, the essential needs are to measure its position with respect to the stars and to find out how it is moving. Only when it has been under observation for some time can a reliable orbit be plotted. Amateurs can contribute by taking photographs of the comet against the stars, but mathematicians must

examine the observations and work on the calculations.
Modern computing machines make the task much
easier, but skill is as necessary as it has ever been.

On the occasions when the moon passes directly in
front of the sun, producing a total eclipse, it is possible
to see the sun's atmosphere: the red chromosphere,
which is a layer of gas above the brilliant surface; the
so-called prominences, once (misleadingly) called "red
flames," also made up of glowing gas; and the superb
pearly corona, the sun's outer atmosphere, which
stretches across the sky. When the last segment of the
sun's disk is hidden, all nature seems to come to a stop.
The sky darkens, and the stars and planets come out.
Only then are we able to see a dark sky with the sun
above the horizon. In 1882, photographs were taken of
a total eclipse which was visible from Egypt. They
showed not only the corona but also a bright comet
quite close to the sun. It had never been seen before,
and it has never been seen again—the photographs are
the only record of it. It is commonly known as Tewfik's
Comet, in honor of Mohammed Tewfik Pasha, then the
ruler of Egypt.

In 1882 photography was in its infancy, astronomically speaking. Should a brilliant comet be seen during
a modern eclipse, it would be widely recorded. However, there is always the chance that a fainter one
would escape notice, because almost everybody would
be concentrating upon the sun itself rather than on
surrounding areas of the sky. During two of the four
total eclipses that I have seen, I have made elaborate
plans for taking sky photographs in the faint hope of
catching an unknown comet. My first attempt—in Si-

beria in 1968—was doomed to failure from the outset; totality lasted for only 37 seconds, and the sky never became really dark. I hoped for better luck during the eclipse of June 30, 1973, which I observed from a ship, the *MS Monte Umbe*, 24 miles off the coast of Mauritania, in Africa. Totality extended over more than 6 minutes, which was practically a record; but unfortunately there was a certain amount of high-altitude haze, and I could see no stars at all, although the planets Venus and Saturn shone out. Under such conditions, it was clearly pointless to search for faint comets, and I contented myself with carrying out a commentary for British television and taking pictures of the corona.

Meanwhile the band of enthusiastic comet hunters will continue its nightly searches. Unfortunately the results mostly will be negative, but if the observer persists long enough, sooner or later he has at least a good chance of discovering a comet. And if so, the sight of the tiny, pale blur of light against the backcloth of remote stars will be full reward for the hundreds of hours of patient work.

5 ENCKE'S COMET AND OTHER FREQUENT VISITORS

In addition to newly discovered comets, several old friends return to perihelion each year. As has been mentioned, few periodic comets can be followed throughout their orbits. Of those that can, the best example is Comet Schwassmann–Wachmann 1, which keeps strictly to the zone between Jupiter and Saturn; another is Gunn's Comet, first seen much more recently (in 1970), whose distance from the sun ranges between about 230 million and 330 million miles, putting it in the region of the asteroid zone.

More than forty short-period comets have now been observed at more than one return, so that their orbits are well known. Some are familiar indeed; Encke's Comet, first seen in 1786 by Pierre Méchain, made its fiftieth appearance in 1973. To describe all short-period comets would be somewhat tedious, so I shall discuss in this chapter mainly those that have been under observation at some time or other during the period 1973–1975. For convenience, these are grouped by year in the tables on pages 56 and 67. I begin with 1973 because during that year several comets of special interest happened to be on view.

The comets in each table are listed chronologically by the date of perihelion. This can be calculated accurately, and so can the period, even though a comet never follows exactly the same orbit twice. The column headed "magnitude," however, needs some explanation.

With the stars, and with the planets, magnitude is a measure of apparent brightness. The scale works in the manner of a golf handicap, with the more brilliant performers having the lower values. Stars of magnitude 6 are just visible to the naked eye on a clear night; those of magnitude 5 are brighter, 4 brighter still, and so on. Really conspicuous stars, such as Altair in the Eagle, are of the first magnitude, and we can even have zero magnitudes or negative values. Sirius, the most brilliant star in the sky, is of magnitude -1.4. Of the planets, Venus can exceed magnitude -4; on the same scale the full moon is about -12, and the sun is -26. Toward the faint end of the scale, binoculars can show stars down to about magnitude $+9$; the powerful telescope in my own observatory will carry me down to $+15$, and the world's greatest telescopes can take photographs of stars as dim as magnitude $+23$.

The scale is satisfactory for stars, which are virtually point sources, and for planets, which show very small disks. For the magnitude of a comet, it is less accurate, because a comet appears as a blur rather than a sharp point. The values given in the tables refer to the nucleus only, so that the comets seem rather more conspicuous than might be expected, although not many of them come within the range of the average amateur-owned telescope.

In the following list, the first three comets had already been recovered by the beginning of 1973; the rest followed in due course. (Gunn's Comet is so faint, except when near perihelion, which it reaches in 1976, that it is included only in the list for 1975.)

Encke's Comet has the longest history, and it is the brightest of the objects in our list (during 1974 it became relatively easy to see). Its story began, so far as we are concerned, on January 17, 1786, when Messier's contemporary Pierre Méchain discovered a telescopic comet in the constellation of Aquarius, the Water Bearer. Méchain immediately sent the news on to Messier, who observed the comet on the first clear night after the announcement. The nucleus was fairly bright, but there was no tail. Since only a few observations were made of the comet, no reliable orbit could be worked out.

SHORT-PERIOD COMETS ON VIEW DURING 1973

Name	Perihelion date	Period (Years)	Maximum magnitude 1973 (Nucleus)
Giacobini–Zinner	August 4, 1972	6.52	17
Tempel 2	November 15, 1972	5.26	18
Kwerns–Kwee	November 29, 1972	9.01	16
Reinmuth 1	March 21, 1973	7.63	17
Tuttle–Giacobini– Kresák	May 29, 1973	5.56	14
Wild	July 2, 1973	13.29	19
Brooks 2	January 4, 1974	6.88	17
Encke	April 28, 1974	3.30	18
Reinmuth 2	May 7, 1974	6.73	19
Borrelly	May 12, 1974	6.77	18
Schwassmann– Wachmann 2	September 12, 1974	6.51	18
Schwassmann– Wachmann 1	———	16.30	18

On November 7, 1795, Caroline Herschel, presumably taking time off from acting as her brother's assistant, discovered a comet which was circular in shape but not well defined. Others also saw it and were puzzled by the way in which it was moving. At this time only Halley's Comet was known to travel around the sun in an ellipse.

On October 19, 1805, the French astronomer Thulis, at Marseilles, found a comet which was just visible with the naked eye. By early November it had developed a short tail, and Johann Encke, director of the Berlin Observatory, tried to work out an orbit for it. He suggested that it might have a period of about twelve years, but he was the first to admit that his value was very uncertain.

The next chapter began on November 26, 1818, when Pons discovered a small, inconspicuous comet without a tail. It remained on view for almost two months, and many careful measurements were made as it tracked slowly against the starry background. Encke gave it his attention and found that no open-curve (parabolic) orbit would fit the observations. Using a new mathematical method, he calculated that the period could be no more than 3.5 years. He then consulted the comet catalogues and found that the orbit was strikingly similar to those of Méchain's comet of 1786, Caroline Herschel's of 1795, and Thulis' of 1805. The identifications could not be regarded as certain, because the earlier comets had been less thoroughly observed (particularly in the case of Méchain's), but Encke was confident enough to predict that there would be another return to perihelion on May 24, 1822.

Astronomers watched. On June 2, 1822, a German astronomer named C. L. Rumker, in Australia, found the comet just where Encke had said it would be, and calculations showed that it really had passed perihelion toward the end of May. Encke at once worked out the time for the next return—September 1825. Again the comet appeared on schedule. Since then it has been missed at only one return: that of 1944, when it was badly placed and when many astronomers had their minds on other things. It is surely fitting to call it Encke's Comet.

When Thulis saw it in 1805, it was visible with the naked eye. At the 1828 return it reached magnitude 5, and when it appeared in 1871 it developed an interesting fanlike tail. Nowadays it is seldom so prominent as this, and I have never personally seen it with the naked eye, nor have I seen a definite tail, although I have looked at it quite often since the 1930s. My observations may not be significant, but there are other suggestions that it is not so bright as it used to be. If so, why not?

Each time a comet comes back to the region of the sun, it loses a little of its substance because the ices in it tend to evaporate. It is estimated that Encke's Comet, which has the shortest period known and which passes through perihelion thirty times in every century, loses 1/200 of its mass at each return. This wastage is quite appreciable, particularly for such a flimsy body as a comet, and it may well be that this old friend is nearing the end of its lifetime. If it can last for 200 returns, it will have been identifiable as a comet for about 660 years. It has been known for almost two centuries now, and we may be watching its gradual demise. There have even been predictions that it will fade away at some time between 1990 and 2000. Personally, I hope that this is not so—the solar system would seem incomplete without it—and yet it cannot persist for very long on the cosmic time scale. In the foreseeable future it must die, as a few former comets (such as Biela's) have already been known to do.

Yet the evidence that Encke's Comet is fading has been challenged. As can be seen from the 1974 table on page 67, its maximum magnitude was then 4; but this is unconfirmed and may be misleading, because when the comet was at its brightest it was hopelessly near the sun. All we can really say is that there is a distinct chance that the comet is decreasing in brilliancy over the years.

Another interesting fact is that the period of Encke's Comet has shortened appreciably. Its distance from the sun ranges between 31.5 million and 381 million miles, so that it travels from near the orbit of Mercury right out into the asteroid belt. (It has sometimes approached within 4 million miles of Mercury.) The period shortened by more than a day between 1822 and 1858, and Encke himself reached the conclusion that when it was near the sun the comet was having to "push through" some resisting medium (that is to say, thin gas), so that it was braked. In fact, this was not the right answer; the process of evaporation is responsible. The effect is particularly noticeable with Encke's Comet because it comes back to the sun so often.

Whether it will continue to hold the "short-period record" remains to be seen. Comet Wilson–Harrington,

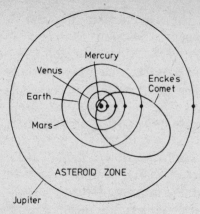

Fig. 8. The orbit of Encke's Comet. At perihelion it is closer to the sun than is Mercury; at aphelion it penetrates the asteroid belt.

discovered in 1949, was calculated to have a period of only 2.3 years, with an orbit taking it from 95,600,000 to 230 million miles from the sun; but it has never been seen again, and it is doubtful it will be recovered. At present, then, Encke's Comet is unchallenged. Its period is more than a year shorter than that of its nearest rival, Grigg–Skjellerup (4.9 years).

I have described Encke's Comet in detail because it is of special interest and importance. The other comets in the 1973 list are always fainter than Encke's at its best, but they too have points of interest, dim and elusive though they undoubtedly are.

Tempel 2 was discovered as long ago as 1873 by Ernst Wilhelm Liebrecht Tempel, a German astronomer living in Italy. (He had found his first periodic comet six years earlier.) Its return in November 1972 was the fourteenth to be observed, but it was badly placed, and excessively faint, during 1973.

The rather picturesquely named comet Kwerns–Kwee has a curious history. It was discovered in 1963 during a search for an entirely different periodic comet which had been lost for some time. The newcomer was found to have formerly had a period of 51 years and to have moved in a path which never brought it anywhere near the earth. A close approach to Jupiter in 1961 completely changed the comet's orbit. Its period was reduced to 5.26 years and it became bright enough to be detected, although it is still very dim. Elizabeth Roemer found it again in July 1971; it was still under observation at the beginning of 1973.

Another 1973 comet which has undergone wild perturbations in its orbit is Brooks 2. It was first seen in July 1889, but its most exciting adventures had occurred three years earlier. What apparently happened was that the comet, which had had a period of 29 years, had a dramatic encounter with Jupiter in March 1886 and actually invaded that planet's system of satellites. Io, the innermost of the four large Jovian moons, travels around the planet at a distance of only 260,000 miles, and Brooks 2 passed closer in than that. In its first orbit it was moving at more than 8 miles per second, but Jupiter "swung it around" and slowed it down. There were two important results. First, the comet's orbit was changed into a much smaller curve with a period of only 6.75 years. Second, the comet itself was damaged, because it had been subjected to tremendous gravitational strain. It must also have penetrated the zones of intense radiation surrounding Jupiter, which were studied in detail by the probes Pioneer 10 in 1973 and Pioneer 11 in 1974.

The effects on the comet were still noticeable in 1889, when Barnard found that it was "multiple," inasmuch as the main object was attended by four companions—splinters, if you like. Two of the splinters soon vanished; then the third expanded and faded away, and finally the fourth lost its tail and faded out in similar fashion. There was no doubt at all that the comet had been in grave danger of total disruption, and for this there was a striking precedent in Biela's Comet, which is described later. Astronomers watched eagerly for the return of Brooks 2 in 1896. It appeared on schedule, and when first seen, by Javelle at Nice on June 20, it was single. Since then it has been observed at every return apart from those of 1918 and 1967, when it was very badly placed. It is, of course, very faint, but after its

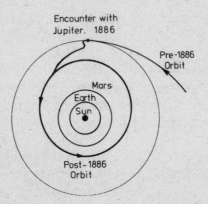

Fig. 9. Changes in the orbit of Comet Brooks 2. In 1886 the comet passed Jupiter and was swung into an orbit of a much shorter period.

devastating experiences near Jupiter, it is lucky to have survived at all.

Incidentally, in spite of its involvement with the Jovian satellite system, Brooks 2 had no measurable effect upon the movements of the satellites themselves. This is extra proof, if proof were needed, of the real flimsiness of a comet. To perturb a satellite such as Io by any detectable amount, the comet's mass would have had to be multiplied by a factor of millions. In 1947 the Russian astronomer N. T. Bobrovnikov tried to work out a reliable value for the density and diameter of another periodic comet, Wolf 1 (see table for 1975), which also had been strongly perturbed by Jupiter. He calculated that the diameter of the nucleus could not be more than 5.5 miles and was probably much less. Encke's Comet may be a little larger, but the values are bound to be arbitrary, because there is as yet no really accurate figure for the density of cometary material. All we can say is that it is very rarefied indeed.

Most of the other short-period comets of 1973 may be passed over with only brief comment. Giacobini–Zinner is interesting because meteors spread along its orbit can occasionally produce major showers, as in 1933. Borrelly's Comet was discovered in 1904 and has been seen at every subsequent return apart from 1939 and 1946. Wild's Comet, with a rather longer period, had been seen for the first time in 1960, so it was making its first predicted return. On the other hand, Schwassmann–Wachmann 2 has never failed to come under observation at each perihelion passage since 1929. It also has had a checkered history; before 1921 its orbit was much more circular than is the case today and its period was over 9 years. As usual, Jupiter provided the disturbing force.

Schwassmann–Wachmann 1, first discovered in 1925, was also on view during 1973. (The cumbersome name of these two comets is due to their discovery by two German astronomers, A. Schwassmann and A. A. Wachmann, working together at the Bergedorf Observatory.) Schwassmann–Wachmann 1 has a really exceptional orbit, more like that of a planet than a comet. There were even some early suggestions that it might be an asteroid, but this is certainly not so. It shows a slight but distinct coma, which no asteroid can do, and it is subject to sudden, unpredictable outbursts which bring it into the range of reasonably small telescopes.

Its distance from the sun was found to range between

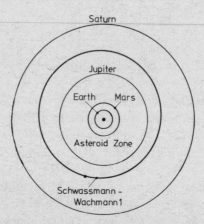

Fig. 10. Orbit of Comet Schwassmann–Wachmann 1. The eccentricity is low, and the comet keeps strictly to the area between the orbits of Jupiter and Saturn, so that it is observable every year.

about 510 million and about 670 million miles; the values for Jupiter and Saturn are, on average, 483 million and 886 million miles respectively, so that Schwassmann–Wachmann 1 kept strictly to the zone between them. The inclination of the orbit was 9.5 degrees and the period rather more than 16 years. This remained the case until the middle of 1974. In June of that year the comet made a close approach to Jupiter, which, as usual, altered its orbit. By 1979 it will be moving in a near-circle, with a distance from the sun ranging between 521 million and 591 million miles.

Generally the magnitude is no brighter than 18, but sometimes a starlike point appears in the nucleus and develops quickly; the brightness increases, and the nucleus expands into a small disk. Slowly the size grows and the brightness drops, until the comet returns to its normal appearance. Obviously, material is being sent outward, and the velocities involved may reach several miles per second. These remarkable outbursts were first studied in detail by the East German astronomer Nikolaus Richter several decades ago. He found that in September 1941 the magnitude rose to 11. There was another flare-up in 1946, observed at Yerkes Observatory, in the United States, by the Belgian-born comet expert George van Biesbroeck. The magnitude was normal at the beginning of the year, but then came the outburst. By January 26 the magnitude was 9.4, almost within binocular range. This meant that the luminosity had increased some 3,000 times. Other sudden rises in brightness occurred in 1959, 1961, and 1965.

Major disturbances have also been seen in other comets, but the behavior of Schwassmann–Wachmann 1 remains in a class of its own, and at the moment no one knows exactly what happens. The other comets with orbits much less eccentric than normal have not been observed to act in comparable fashion. Gunn's does not; neither did Oterma's, which used to move in a more or less circular path, although in 1965 it was perturbed by Jupiter and thrown into its present orbit of greater ellipticity and a period of 19 years.

As has been noted, Schwassmann–Wachmann 1 can be kept under observation all the time except when it is too close to the sun. It is usually much too faint to be detectable with modest equipment, but checks on its position are given in various annual publications.

Now let us consider the lists for 1974 and 1975. I have omitted Westphal's Comet, which did not appear in 1975. It had a longer period (61 years), but it has never been recovered. Schwassmann–Wachmann 1 is omitted from both the 1974 and 1975 lists.

Several of these comets had not been seen since the year of their discovery. This was 1906 in the case of Metcalf's Comet, which, according to calculation, passed near Jupiter in 1911, 1935, and again in 1969, with consequent disturbances in its orbit; Swift 2 had been untracked since 1895. In contrast is Finlay's Comet, originally seen by the astronomer of that name from the Cape Observatory in 1886. Its movement is well known, and it has been seen regularly; the 1974 perihelion passage was the thirteenth on record. The career of Comet Wolf 1 has already been mentioned. I must emphasize the fact that the maximum magnitude of Encke's Comet took place when the sun was too close in the sky to allow the comet to be seen, so that the

SHORT-PERIOD COMETS ON VIEW DURING 1974

Name	Perihelion date	Period (Years)	Maximum magnitude 1974 (Nucleus)
Reinmuth 2	May 7, 1974	6.73	17
Borrelly	May 12, 1974	6.77	17
Schwassmann–Wachmann 2	September 12, 1974	6.51	17
Encke	April 28, 1974	3.30	4
Brooks 2	January 4, 1974	6.88	18
Schwassmann–Wachmann 3	March 17, 1974	5.40	18
Du Toit 1	April 4, 1974	14.96	17
Forbes	May 20, 1974	6.40	14
Finlay	July 12, 1974	6.95	14
Honda–Mrkós–Pajdusáková	December 28, 1974	5.28	13
Swift 2	November 5, 1974	7.15	18

SHORT-PERIOD COMETS ON VIEW DURING 1975

Name	Perihelion date	Period (Years)	Maximum magnitude 1975 (Nucleus)
Schwassmann–Wachmann 2	September 12, 1974	6.51	17
Honda–Mrkós–Pajdusáková	December 28, 1974	5.28	12
Arend	May 25, 1975	7.89	19
Metcalf	June 20, 1975	7.77	18
Perrine–Mrkós	August 2, 1975	6.78	15
Giacobini	November 7, 1975	6.61	18
Wolf 1	January 25, 1976	8.42	18
Gunn	February 11, 1976	6.81	16
Harrington–Abell	April 21, 1976	7.58	18

value is theoretical only. On the whole, the lists for 1974 and 1975 are less interesting than that for 1973.

A few other short-period comets have been seen regularly for many years. Faye's, first detected in 1843, came back on schedule once more at the end of 1976. Yet of all the flock there are very few that ever come within the range of small telescopes. A bright comet every few years would be welcome, but Nature does not oblige us, and the only comet with a period of less than a century which can be relied upon to make a brave showing is Halley's, which is the subject of the next chapter.

6 HALLEY'S COMET

Of all the comets in the sky,
There's none like Comet Halley.
We see it with the naked eye,
And periodically.

The authorship of this immortal verse is obscure; it was certainly not written by Shakespeare, but it is the sort of jingle which sticks in one's head. Halley's Comet is indeed unique; it can become striking, and there is no doubt that it will be found again as it comes in toward its next perihelion in 1986.

On August 15, 1682, a comet was recorded by a German astronomer named Georg Samuel Dorffel. It was also seen at the relatively new observatory at Greenwich, England, and some observations of it were made by the Astronomer Royal, John Flamsteed. Another man who looked at it attentively was Edmond Halley, later to succeed Flamsteed at Greenwich. (The correct spelling of Halley's first name is Edmond, not Edmund. The scientific historian Colin Ronan maintains that "Halley" should rhyme with "poorly," not "valley," which would, alas, ruin the verse at the opening of this chapter.)

The head of the 1682 comet became really bright, and its tail extended some distance across the sky. Various drawings of it were made—one by Johannes

Hevelius of Danzig (modern Gdańsk), a leading observer of the period. The drawings were somewhat peculiar, but they showed that the comet was very prominent indeed.

At this time, comets were not considered members of the solar system. (Kepler, as noted earlier, had believed that they traveled in straight lines and did not obey the laws of planetary motion.) Halley, a close friend of Isaac Newton, who was then working on the theories of gravitation, began to wonder whether the 1682 comet was periodic and had been seen at earlier returns.

Halley waited until Newton's new theories had become established, and then he set to work. Using Flamsteed's observations and those of other astronomers, he calculated the orbit of the 1682 comet as carefully as he could and found that the measured positions would fit an assumed period of around 75 years. He then checked back to see what other comets of similar brilliancy had been seen in the past. Among them were comets which had been under observation for some time in 1607 and in 1531. The intervals between perihelion passages were not exactly equal, but Halley found that between 1607 and 1682 the comet must have passed close enough to Jupiter for its period to be appreciably shortened. Before long he had come to the firm conclusion that the three comets—1531, 1607, and 1682—were one and the same.

His results were communicated to Britain's senior scientific organization, the Royal Society, in 1705. He wrote in Latin. A translation of the relevant part of his paper follows.

Now many things lead me to believe that the comet of the year 1531, observed by Apian, is the same as that which in the year 1607 was described by Kepler and Longomontanus, and which I myself saw and observed at its return in 1682. All the elements agree, except that there is an inequality in the times of revolution; but this is not so great that it cannot be attributed to physical causes. For example, the motion of Saturn is so disturbed by the other planets, and especially by Jupiter, that its periodic time is uncertain to the extent of several days. How much more liable to such perturbations is a comet which recedes to a distance nearly four times greater than that to Saturn, and a slight increase in whose velocity could change its orbit from an ellipse into a parabola! The identity of these comets is confirmed by the fact that in 1456 a comet was seen, which passed in a retrograde direction between the earth and the sun, in nearly the same manner; and although it was not observed astronomically, yet from its period and its path I infer that it was the same comet as that of the years 1531, 1607, and 1682. I may, therefore, with confidence predict its return in the year 1758. If this prediction is fulfilled, there is no reason to doubt that other comets will return.

He added, modestly, that if he were proved right, posterity would not fail to acknowledge that the discovery had first been made by an Englishman.

Halley, who was born in 1656, could not hope to live to see his prediction fulfilled; in fact he died in 1742. Later, some new calculations w̲ French astronomers, Lalande, Al̲ and Madame Nicole Lepaute. when Messier, among others, h̲ search, Clairaut announced that the comet for 100 days and Jupiter for 518 days, so that the actual date of perihelion would be in the spring of 1759. Yet Halley was vindicated in every respect. On Christmas night, 1758, a German amateur, Johann Georg Palitzsch, duly picked up the comet; Messier saw it on January 21, 1759, and it passed through perihelion on March 12. Extensive observations of it were made by astronomers all over the world.

By common consent Halley's name was attached to the comet, and surely the honor was well deserved. His investigation was something entirely new, and it showed, for the first time, that some comets at least had to be ranked as true members of the solar system.

The next return was due in 1835, and astronomers began looking for it well ahead of time; by then they knew more or less what to expect. Apparently the first observation was made on August 6, 1835, by the Frenchman M. Dumouchel, from Rome; the comet was seen as a dim, misty patch near the star Zeta Tauri, not far from the brilliant orange-red Aldebaran, or "Eye of the Bull." As the comet neared the sun it brightened and developed a major tail; it passed through perihelion in November, and although it faded quickly it was followed telescopically until May of the following year. The last observation made of it was due to Sir John Herschel (son of Sir William), from his temporary observatory at the Cape of Good Hope, where he had gone to study the stars of the far south. Of course, this was in the pre-photographic era, but faithful drawings of the comet were made.

The most recent return was that of 1910. Very exact alculations of the path had been made by two Greenwich astronomers, A. C. D. Crommelin and Philip Cowell, so that the comet was found early; it was detected on September 12, 1909, by Max Wolf in Germany, when it was still over 300 million miles from the sun—that is to say, well out in the asteroid zone, beyond Mars. (This statement, however, applies only in the sense of distance. The orbital inclination of the comet is very high, so that it avoids the main asteroid swarm. It also moves in a retrograde direction, unlike any known asteroid.) It passed perihelion on schedule, within three days of the time given by Crommelin and Cowell, and it remained under observation until June 1911, when its distance from the sun had grown to more than 500 million miles—greater than the mean distance of Jupiter.

There were two points of special interest connected with this return. On May 18/19 Halley's Comet passed directly between the earth and the sun, and astronomers were anxious to know whether any sign of the event could be seen; the American astronomer Ferdinand Ellerman made a trip to Hawaii to observe under the best possible conditions. He could see no trace of the comet in front of the sun, which was an extra confirmation of the flimsiness of cometary material. Also, the earth passed through the outer edge of the comet's tail, again without any visible result (although it is true that at the time the nucleus of the comet was still millions of miles away).

Over the years I have had many letters from people who tell me that they have vivid memories of Halley's Comet in 1910 and look forward to seeing it once more in 1986. Unfortunately, most of these accounts proba-

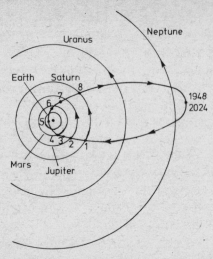

Fig. 11. Orbit of Halley's Comet. At perihelion the distance of the comet from the sun is less than that of the earth; at aphelion the comet recedes well beyond Neptune. The positions from 1983 to 1988 are shown. (1) mid-1983; (2) late winter 1985; (3) summer 1985; (4) winter 1985; (5) February 5, 1986; (6) spring 1986; (7) autumn 1986; (8) summer 1988. Perihelion will take place in 1986; the last aphelion was in 1948, and the next will be in 2024.

bly do not relate to Halley's Comet at all. Earlier in 1910 a much brighter, nonperiodic comet had come into view; it became visible with the naked eye even with the sun above the horizon, so that it is remembered as the Daylight Comet. Since it was far more brilliant than Halley's, I suspect that this is the object remembered by most of my correspondents, particularly as Halley's showed at its best from the southern hemisphere. Actually the Daylight Comet has been the most spectacular of the century so far.

At the 1910 return, Halley's Comet was picked up seven months before perihelion. The next return to perihelion is due in February 1986 (preliminary calculations give the date as February 5), which means that it should be found in the middle of 1985. It must have passed aphelion in 1948—at a distance of 3,300 million miles, well beyond the path of Neptune. It is now drawing steadily closer to the earth and is speeding up.

Just how brilliant Halley's Comet will become in 1986 remains to be seen. Quite possibly it is not now so spectacular as it used to be long ago, because it, like all other periodic comets, must suffer appreciable wastage of material every time it passes perihelion and develops a tail. However, its "life expectancy" must be long in comparison with that of Encke's, which is smaller and returns more often, and we cannot be certain that there has been a measurable fading.

Records of this comet go back a very long way. The ancient Chinese were careful observers (even though they had no idea what a comet was), and it is possible that a comet recorded by them in 467 B.C. was Halley's. The identification with the comet of 240 B.C. is slightly more definite. There are no reports of the return which presumably took place in 163 B.C., but it came back again in 11 B.C., and since then it has been seen each time it has passed through perihelion: in A.D. 66, 141, 218, 295, 373, 451, 530, 607–608 (two bright comets were seen then, and we cannot be sure which was Halley's), 683, 760, 837, 912, 989, 1066, 1145, 1223, 1301, 1378, 1456, and then, as already discussed, in 1531, 1607, 1682, 1759, 1835, and 1910. It has not always been brilliant; from all reports it made a poor showing in 1145 and in 1378 but was much more striking in 1301 and in 1456, the year when Pope Calixtus III was supposed to have excommunicated it as an agent of the devil. The first known drawing of it refers to the return of 684 and comes from the *Nürnberg Chronicle,* although I would hate to suggest that the representation is really faithful.

One celebrated return was that of 1066. The comet is said to have alarmed the Saxon court, and there is a representation of it in the Bayeux Tapestry, which some authorities believe to have been woven by William the Conqueror's wife. If the scene is authentic, King Harold is certainly toppling on his throne! There is no doubt whatever that the 1066 comet really was Halley's.

A further interesting sidelight on this extraordinary comet is the fact that it may provide a clue to a problem which has concerned many astronomers in recent years. This is the possible existence of a tenth planet in the solar system.

I have already mentioned that each planet pulls upon its fellows, producing what are called perturbations. Earth's movement is affected by Venus, Mars, Jupiter, and so on; if these planets did not exist, Earth's orbit around the sun would not be quite the same as it actually is. The perturbations can be worked out very exactly and can be allowed for. It was through such calculations that the two outermost planets, Neptune and Pluto, were tracked down before they were seen telescopically.

The story really began in 1781, when William Herschel, then only an unknown amateur, was carrying

out a "review of the heavens" with a homemade reflecting telescope. In checking the stars in the constellation of Gemini (the Twins), he came across an object
which looked quite unlike a star. It showed a definite
disk, which no star does, and it was in motion. Herschel
believed it to be a comet, and indeed his original report
to the Royal Society was headed "An Account of a
Comet." Before long, however, it became clear that the
object was a new giant planet moving well beyond the
orbit of Saturn, up to then the most distant known body
in the solar system. The new planet was named Uranus,
and Herschel's reputation was established.

The mathematicians promptly set out to calculate
the way in which Uranus should move. Alas, it refused
to behave. It persistently wandered from its predicted
path, and eventually astronomers began to wonder
whether it could be affected by yet another planet,
farther away from the sun and as yet unknown. Careful
calculations were made independently by Urbain Le
Verrier in France and by John Couch Adams in England. Their results agreed well, and in 1846 the predicted planet was found very close to the position
which had been given.

With Neptune, as the newcomer was named, the solar system again seemed to be complete, but there were
still some very slight irregularities unaccounted for. In
the early part of the twentieth century the American
astronomer Percival Lowell, best remembered today
for his admittedly rather wild theories about the "ca-
nals" on Mars, carried through a similar sort of investigation and arrived at a position for a ninth planet. From
his observatory at Flagstaff, Arizona, he searched for it

but failed to find it, and after his death in 1916 the search was temporarily given up. Then, in 1930, a young astronomer at the Lowell Observatory—Clyde Tombaugh, who is still living—achieved success. He tracked down a very faint, starlike object which proved to be the long-awaited planet. It was named Pluto.

The reason Lowell failed was that Pluto was much fainter than expected; a fairly powerful telescope is needed to show it, and it is a relatively small body, almost certainly much less massive than Earth. This set theorists a strange problem. A planet as small as Pluto could not produce any noticeable perturbations in the motions of giants such as Uranus and Neptune, and yet it was by these very perturbations that Pluto had been located. Something was wrong somewhere. Either the discovery had been sheer luck, or Pluto must be much more massive than it seemed, or—just possibly—Pluto was not "Lowell's planet" at all, in which case another one awaited discovery.

Certainly Pluto is an odd kind of planet. Its orbital inclination is 17 degrees, much more than that of any other principal planet, and its path is so eccentric that it can come within the orbit of Neptune, as shown in Fig. 12. For some years on either side of its next perihelion passage (due in 1989) it will forfeit its title of "the outermost world." It is a slow mover, taking more than 247 years to complete one journey around the sun. Recent investigations show that the surface of Pluto is covered with methane ice.

Pluto is so great an enigma that it may not even be a true planet at all; the suggestion that it may be an ex-satellite of Neptune has much to recommend it. It is

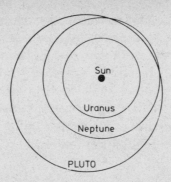

Fig. 12. The orbit of Pluto, which is relatively eccentric and inclined. At perihelion the distance from the sun is less than that of Neptune, but there is no fear of collision because Pluto's path is tilted at an angle of 17 degrees. The next perihelion is due in 1989.

probably not much larger than Triton, the first discovered of Neptune's two present-day satellites.

Under the circumstances, the possibility of another true planet seems very reasonable. The main difficulty is that, even if such a planet exists, it will be extremely faint. Without a really good idea of its position, finding it will be purely a matter of luck, and a systematic search would tie up a very large telescope for a very long time, with no guarantee of success in the end. In 1972 Dr. Joseph Brady, of the United States, approached the problem from a different angle. Instead of considering the possible effects of an unknown body upon the known planets, he concentrated upon the movements of Halley's Comet.

From the reliable measurements made in 1835 and particularly in 1910, the orbit of the comet is now very well known. Working from this, Brady published a paper in which he discussed some minor irregularities and suggested that these were due to the hypothetical planet. His specifications were surprising. The planet was supposed to be a giant, with a mass three times that of Saturn, a period of 512 years, a distance from the sun more than twice that of Neptune—and retrograde motion. The orbital inclination was said to be as much as 60 degrees.

The position of the planet, as given by Brady for early 1972, was in the northern constellation of Cassiopeia, whose five main stars make up a rough **W** or **M** shape, and which is familiar to anyone who has even the most rudimentary knowledge of the sky. Cassiopeia lies a long way from the zodiac and would be the last place in which anyone would normally think of searching for a major planet. If the object were as bright as Brady believed (magnitude 14 to 15), it would be within the range of moderate equipment, and many people, including myself, carried out prompt and systematic searches. The results were entirely negative, and I think it is now fair to say that no planet of this brightness exists close to the Brady position. Since then, fresh calculations made elsewhere have cast serious doubt upon the whole investigation. Certainly a giant planet moving in a highly tilted, wrong-way path seems highly improbable.

There, for the moment, the matter rests. Planet Ten may or may not exist. Whether Halley's Comet can provide any vital clues remains to be seen, but its next return should produce answers of some kind.

This chapter has concentrated on Halley's Comet, but various others with periods of between 60 and 155 years have been observed at more than one return (see Appendix, Table I). However, since none of these can ever become brilliant, interest in them is mainly restricted to cometary enthusiasts; the average sky watcher will not be greatly concerned. But there can be no doubt that everyone will be excited about the return of Halley's Comet as it swings back once more in the latter part of 1985.

7 GREAT COMETS

Although spectacular comets have been rare in this century, they have been seen often enough in the past. Many of the early descriptions cannot be taken at face value, although some are straightforward enough; there is little doubt that the comet of 1264 had a tail which stretched more than halfway across the sky. On the other hand there are accounts such as that written about the comet of 1528 by the French physician Ambroise Paré:

This comet was so horrible, so frightful, and it produced such great terror that some died of fear and others fell sick. It appeared to be of extreme length, and was of the color of blood. At the summit of it was seen the figure of a bent arm, holding in its hand a great sword as if about to strike. At the end of the point there were three stars. On both sides of the rays of this comet were seen a great number of axes, knives, and blood-colored swords, among which were a large number of hideous human faces, with beards and bristling hair.

One would suspect that Dr. Paré was less reliable astronomically than he is known to have been in his own profession of medicine. There is even doubt as to whether the phenomenon he describes was a comet: suggestions have been made that what he saw was really a brilliant display of aurora borealis (Northern

Lights). In any case, his description shows comets were not welcome visitors.

At least there is no doubt about the comet of 1680, which was discovered by the German astronomer Gottfried Kirch at Coburg. The tail was at one time 90 degrees long, and the nucleus was brilliant. This, incidentally, was the comet that so alarmed the Reverend William Whiston.

The comet of 1744 was discovered on December 9, 1743, by Klinkenberg in Holland and was seen four days later by De Chéseaux in Switzerland; rather unfairly, it is always known as De Chéseaux's Comet. It must have been one of the most spectacular ever observed, because apparently it had at least half a dozen bright, broad tails. We have a good idea of what it looked like, because De Chéseaux himself left a drawing, made when the actual head of the comet was below

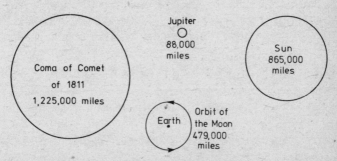

Fig. 13. The size of the coma of the Great Comet of 1811 compared with the diameters of the sun and Jupiter and the orbit of the moon. Despite its great size, the mass of the Comet of 1811 was negligible by planetary standards.

the horizon so that the tails swept upward in the manner of a fan. Unfortunately there are not many records
of the comet, and it seems to have remained brilliant
only for a night or two in early March. Obviously we
know nothing precise about its orbit, but it must certainly have a period so long that it will not return for
many centuries, if at all.

The Great Comet of 1811 has one distinction: it
seems to have had the largest coma ever recorded. At
maximum its diameter was of the order of 1.25 million
miles, so that it was considerably larger than the sun
even though its mass was so slight. Around October
1811 the tail extended over 100 million miles, with a
breadth of 15 million miles. It was under observation
for some time; it was discovered by the French astronomer Honoré Flaugergues on March 26, 1811, and the
last record of it was obtained by Wisniewski, from
Russia, on August 17, 1812.

The orbit was studied by Friedrich Wilhelm August
Argelander, a famous German astronomer, who
worked out the period as being 3,065 years. Argelander
confidently claimed that his estimate was correct to
within 50 years either way. I have my doubts. While I
will not be able to check on the prediction in A.D. 4876,
when the comet will return if Argelander's calculations
are right, presumably astronomers of that period will
keep a careful watch.

As a casual aside, 1811 was also a year in which the
port wine vintage in Portugal was unusually good. For
years afterward, "Comet Wine" was featured in the
price lists of wine merchants, and advertisements of it
continued until 1880. Whether any "Comet Wine" re-

mains to be drunk today is, I suppose, problematical.

The only comet of near-modern times which sur-passed that of 1811 was the one of 1843. This seems definite, because a celebrated observer, the Irish as-tronomer Thomas Maclear, saw both and wrote that the comet of 1811 "was not half so brilliant as the late one." The tail also was longer, attaining a record length of 200 million miles. According to the descriptions given at the time, the tail was comparatively straight. The comet was what is called a "sun grazer," and at perihelion it passed within about 100,000 miles of the brilliant solar surface, so that it must have been in-

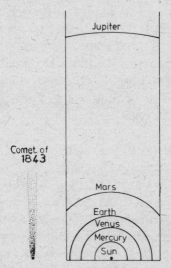

Fig. 14. Length of the tail of the Great Comet of 1843 compared with the orbits of the planets.

tensely heated. It was, of course, visible in daylight, and its orbit was practically or entirely parabolic.

Next in the list of remarkable comets comes Donati's of 1858—possibly the most beautiful ever seen, because of its wonderfully curved main tail and its two shorter ones. Donati, at Florence, discovered it on June 2, 1858; it remained a naked-eye object for over three months and was visible telescopically until March 4, 1859. On October 5, 1858, it passed straight in front of the brilliant star Arcturus—and Arcturus shone as brightly as usual; the flimsy material of the comet was quite unable to dim it. The tail grew from a length of 14 million miles in late August to a maximum of over 50 million miles in October, after which the length began to decrease.

Donati's Comet was not a sun grazer, and even at its closest approach it was still farther out than Mercury. Its main claim to fame, apart from its beauty, is that obvious disturbances took place in its tail. Circular "envelopes" appeared outside the nucleus and seemed to send out masses of brilliant matter which passed down the tail and distorted it.

It is a tremendous pity that this comet made its entry and its exit before the development of reliable astronomical photography. Whether it will ever return we do not know, but there are suggestions that it may have a period of around 2,000 years. One mathematician, Kritzinger, suggested that it might be identical with a great comet recorded by the Roman writer Seneca as having appeared in 146 B.C., but we cannot be sure.

Three years after Donati's Comet, in 1861, came the great comet discovered by an Australian amateur named Jerome Loggia Tebbutt. It was then of magnitude 4, but it brightened quickly. It may not have had the surpassing beauty of Donati's Comet, but according to Sir John Herschel it was decidedly more brilliant, with a complex nucleus and an extremely long tail. There is no doubt that in late June the tail swept over the earth, which for some time was actually inside a comet, although most people were blissfully unaware of the fact. The earth did not pass through the coma, but the minimum distance of the head was only about 11 million miles.

I have combed through papers and accounts written at the time in an effort to see whether anyone noticed anything unusual. The best testimony seems to come from a meteorologist, E. J. Lowe, who claimed that the sky had a strange yellow appearance on the evening of June 30, 1861, and that the brightness of the sun was diminished; in his parish church, the vicar had the pulpit candles lighted at 7 o'clock. Lowe also mentioned that the comet looked hazier than on any other evening. So far as I know, this comet was the first to be the subject of attention from an astronomical photographer. One of the great pioneers, the English astronomer Warren de la Rue, tried to record it with his primitive equipment, although unfortunately without success.

The other bright comets of the later nineteenth century can be noted briefly. The Great Comet of 1862, discovered by Lewis Swift, did not equal that of the previous year but was nevertheless striking and was notable for the luminous jet which came from its nucleus. Coggia's Comet of 1874 (discovered by French

astronomer J. E. Coggia) was also brilliant, and so was
the comet of 1880, which was seen best from the southern hemisphere. The comet of 1882 rivaled any of its
predecessors and was excellently photographed by the
British astronomer Sir David Gill from the Cape of
Good Hope—the first good comet picture ever obtained. At one stage, according to several observers,
including Barnard and Brooks, the comet threw off a
mass of luminous material which gave a temporary impression of being a satellite comet.

There was an important sequel to Gill's work. When
he photographed the comet, he also recorded many
stars. This made him aware of the potential value of
stellar photography and in time led to the compilation
of the photographic star atlases which have now completely replaced the older methods of star cataloging.

The last fairly brilliant comet of the nineteenth century was discovered in 1887 by Paysandu in South
America, who also found another in 1901. Both were
seen best from the southern hemisphere. Accounts of
the comet of 1901 say that it was distinctly yellowish in
color. Then came the Daylight Comet, discovered by
some diamond miners in the Transvaal in South Africa,
on January 12, 1910. Needless to say, they were not
looking for comets, but they could hardly overlook this
one. By January 21 it was well visible from England,
and I quote from a description given by E. Hawkes,
observing from Leeds, England:

The comet was picked up with the naked eye at 4h 40m,
and was a gorgeous object. The picture presented in the
western sky was one which will never be forgotten. A beauti-

ful sunset had just taken place, and a long, low-lying strip of purple cloud stood out in bold relief against the glorious primrose of the sky behind. Away to the right the horizon was topped by a perfectly cloudless sky of turquoise blue, which seemed to possess an unearthly light like that of the aurora borealis. High up in the south-west shone the planet Venus, resplendently brilliant, while below, and somewhat to the right, was the great comet itself, shining with a fiery golden light, its great tail stretching some seven or eight degrees above it. The tail was beautifully curved like a scimitar, and dwindled away into tenuity so that one could not exactly see where it ended. The nucleus was very bright, and seemed to vary. One minute it would be as bright as Mars in opposition, while at another it was estimated to be four times as bright. The tail, too, seemed to pulsate rapidly from the finest veil possible to a sheaf of fiery mist.

No doubt these apparent fluctuations were due to conditions in the earth's atmosphere, but the description is graphic, and it agrees excellently with the account given to me years ago by my colleague the late H. P. Wilkins, who saw the comet from Wales at about the same time. There is no doubt that it was far superior to Halley's, which appeared later in the same year, but Halley's is a regular visitor, while the Daylight Comet will not be seen again in our time.

After 1910 there was a long hiatus, although Skjellerup's Comet of 1927 (named for the Danish astronomer) was bright for a few nights as seen from the southern hemisphere. Other brief visitors were the comets of 1947 and 1948, both of which were bright and had long tails. The 1948 comet was discovered during a total eclipse, seen from Africa, but by the time it came

into view in the northern hemisphere it had faded tre-
mendously.

There have been, of course, naked-eye comets of
lesser splendor. I well remember Finsler's of 1937 and
Comet Jurlov–Achmarov–Hassell of 1939, which had a
pronounced greenish hue. But northern observers had
to wait until 1957, when there came two comets, both
nonperiodic. By no stretch of the imagination could
either be called great, but they were bright enough to
cause general interest even among non-astronomers.

The first of these was discovered by two Belgian astronomers, L. Arend and G. Roland. It was easy to see
with the naked eye, and when I looked at it with
binoculars, in late April, its tail was splendidly displayed. Perhaps I should say "tails," because ahead of
the comet there could be seen a remarkable spike. Actually, this was due to thinly spread material lying in
the plane of the comet's orbit; the material was much
too diffuse to be easily visible far from the head when
seen broadside on, but when the layer was seen "from
the edge" it gave the false impression of a sunward tail.
Comet Arend–Roland had a nucleus which reached the
first magnitude, and it remained on view telescopically
for some months. In August 1957 another fairly bright
comet made its entry; it was discovered by the Czech
astronomer Antonín Mrkós, and it too became conspicuous to the naked eye, although it lacked any spiked
appearance and remained prominent for only a relatively brief period in the morning sky.

At that time it seemed reasonable to hope that the
barren years were over and new bright comets would
appear. Seki–Lines, in 1962, made a brief showing.

Pereyra's, of 1963, would have been classed as great but for the fact that it was never well placed and came nowhere near the earth, so that its glory was completely lost. Then came Ikeya–Seki of 1965, discovered by two of the energetic Japanese searchers on the morning of October 21. Amateur and professional observers all over the world were very much on the alert, since one magnitude estimate had been given as −9, in which case the comet would have been by far the most brilliant since 1910. Undoubtedly it was a sun grazer, and there had even been a suggestion from the Moscow astronomer B. Y. Levin that it would actually hit the sun.

Needless to say, this announcement sparked off all kinds of rumors. One "expert" claimed that the result of such a collision would be to disrupt television reception; the editors of a London daily paper published a spectacular picture of what they believed to be the comet but was in fact an aircraft condensation trail. Subsequently Levin changed his mind and announced that the comet would miss the sun by a small margin, although it might be disrupted by the intense heat.

At this time I was director of the Armagh Planetarium in Northern Ireland. Since the sky was cloudy, I prevailed upon the Royal Air Force to take me up in a high-flying aircraft. From a vantage point above the clouds I hoped to obtain good photographs, but the comet obstinately refused to show itself. Dr. D. W. Dewhirst of Cambridge University was similarly unsuccessful from an aircraft over southern England, even though the comet was then scheduled to be at its best as it emerged from behind the sun. Naturally, we were disappointed, but it then transpired that once again northern-hemisphere observers had been unlucky. Toward the end of October and the beginning of November magnificent views were obtained from South Africa, South America, Australia, and parts of the United States, and there is no doubt that the comet was a great one, with a brilliant head and a long, slightly curved tail, extending to over 30 degrees. It was even said to be comparable with the great comet of 1882. Considerable activity took place in the nucleus around the time of perihelion, and some observers said that when it emerged from the sun's rays it had a distinctly yellowish hue. At its minimum distance from the sun it was a mere 307,000 miles from the solar surface, and spectroscopic examination showed the presence of atoms of sodium, iron, nickel, copper, calcium, and other elements, but the familiar signs of molecules were lacking, since the molecules, which are groups of atoms, had been broken up by the intense heat.

Another Japanese-found comet, Tago–Sato–Kosaka of early 1970, was rather disappointing as a spectacle but had scientific importance because of the discovery that it was enveloped in a huge cloud of rarefied hydrogen. It was followed in the spring by something really worth seeing—the comet which had been discovered late in the previous year by Jack Bennett at Pretoria. When at its very best, Bennett's Comet was well south of the equator of the sky, but it was still bright when it came northward, and I had some splendid views of it from my observatory at Selsey, in Sussex, England, throughout April. Both types of tail were displayed; the 19-degree-long curved tail made of dust, and the shorter, straight tail composed of gas. Spiral-shaped jets were seen in the nucleus, and the whole comet showed marked activity. It too was enveloped in a hydrogen cloud, and the diameter of this cloud seems to have been about 8 million miles, although of course the material was not visible telescopically.

In early April I estimated the magnitude of the nucleus as 1.2, slightly brighter than the star Deneb in Cygnus. Even then it was fading, and by now it has long since disappeared altogether; it has begun its long journey back into the depths of space, and we will not see it again.

I have left almost until last a comet which promised to be great but failed to come up to expectations as a spectacle, although from the scientific point of view it was of special importance. This is Kohoutek's Comet, which caused a tremendous amount of general excitement as it approached the sun and the earth throughout 1973.

It was discovered on March 7, 1973, by Dr. Lubos Kohoutek, a Czechoslovakian astronomer who works at the Hamburg Observatory in West Germany. The circumstances were distinctly unusual. Dr. Kohoutek was looking for a faint periodic comet, Biela's, which had not been seen since 1852 and which has almost certainly broken up. When he developed his plates, Dr. Kohoutek found a comet which was certainly not Biela's and which he soon realized was something unusual. It was faint, with clear indications of a coma. The exceptional thing about it was its distance; over 400 million miles from the earth and over 430 million miles from the sun. Few comets this far out are visible, so the newcomer was obviously very large.

Further calculations made the outlook seem even more promising. During much of the summer the comet would be on the far side of the sun, but it would emerge into the morning sky during October and would cross the earth's orbit in November, although at that time the earth would be some distance away. Predictions were that it would become a naked-eye object in November and that at its brightest it would attain a magnitude of something like −12, comparable with the full moon. This would, of course, make it a daylight object, comparable with any of the comets of past years. At perihelion, on December 28, 1973, it would be racing along at about 100 miles per second (as against the modest 18.5 miles per second, or 66,000 miles per hour, of the earth) and it would pass to within 13 million miles of the sun itself. After perihelion, when it had come into the evening sky, it would still be magnificent and would pass the earth at about 75 million miles in mid-January 1974. It was not expected to fade below naked-eye visibility until the end of February, and it was expected to develop a really long tail. Writers went so far as to refer to it as "the comet of the century."

Astrologers and their kind were in full cry at an early stage, and all sorts of predictions were made. The religious tract mentioned in Chapter 1, which was put out by an organization calling itself the Children of God and which was written by a Mr. Moses David, referred to the announcement of the comet as "shocking" and claimed that the maximum brightness would be seven times as great as that of the moon. In his writing, entitled *The Christmas Monster,* Mr. David went so far as to ask whether the apparition heralded the end of "Fascist America and its new Nazi Emperor," and a few remaining end-of-the-worlders also voiced their apprehensions. Scientists approached the matter differently. It was thought possible that Kohoutek's Comet came from a "comet cloud" orbiting the sun at a distance of about one light-year (roughly 5,800 billion miles) and was paying its first visit to the sun, after a journey lasting for 2 million years. If so, then it would be very "dusty," since it would never before have suffered evaporation of the material in the nucleus under the influence of solar heat.

But as October passed by, doubts developed as to whether Kohoutek would prove brilliant after all. The magnitude was very much below the predicted value, and the tail was negligible. Though low in the dawn sky, it was seen in the right position; but from my Selsey observatory I failed to see it until November 17, when I estimated the magnitude as 7 and found that there was only a trace of a tail, even though I was using my 15-inch reflector, which by amateur standards is powerful. By the end of November the magnitude had increased to 6, and there was a 0.25-degree tail. Observers in clearer climates were able to follow it through most of December, when the tail had grown to more than 10 degrees in length even though it was not brilliant. So far as I know, Jack Bennett, from Pretoria, was the last to see it before its perihelion passage on December 28; his last view was on the 22nd, when it was very low in the dawn glare. There was certainly no chance of its being glimpsed in daylight, as the comets of 1811, 1843, 1861, 1910, and others had been.

During early January 1974 it reappeared in the evening sky, but it was still disappointing, and by now
members of the general public were becoming sadly
disillusioned. I had my best view of it on January 10—
not from my home, but from an aircraft flying at 33,000
feet above the Irish Sea. True, the brilliant planets Venus and Jupiter, together with the comet, made a fascinating spectacle; but the magnitude of the comet was
below 3, and the tail cannot have been more than 10
degrees long, so far as I could judge. By the end of
January the comet had fallen well below naked-eye
visibility, and it continued to fade, although it was followed telescopically for many months.

Yet the view from above the earth's atmosphere was
very different, and fortunately this was the time when
the United States vehicle Skylab was manned by its last
crew—Astronauts Gerald Carr, Edward Gibson, and
William Pogue. During a space walk outside their craft,
only a day after the comet passed perihelion, they had
an excellent view from their vantage point some 270
miles above the ground. There was a distinct tail and a
sunward "spike" recalling Arend–Roland of 1957. Dr.
Gibson described it as "awe-inspiring," with an exceptionally bright nucleus and an overall orange color, although before perihelion it had been white.

As the astronauts continued their studies, the sunward spike grew fainter day by day; the color changed
to light yellow, and the tail length varied, reaching a
maximum of 8 degrees (so that my own value of 10
degrees was probably an overestimate). The fluctuations in tail length were not real but were due to the
changing angle from which the comet was being ob-

served. On one occasion Gibson compared the appearance with that of the plume of a high-altitude rocket exhaust, which certainly gives a good idea of what it must have been like. Between six and nine days after perihelion the color became violet, presumably because the astronauts were now seeing the gas in the tail rather than the dust.

There was, indeed, a great deal of dusty material, as both earth-based and space observations showed, but observers experienced one major disappointment. Researchers at the United States National Radio Astronomy Observatory at Green Bank, West Virginia, used the 36-foot radio telescope to search for various molecules in the cometary material, but unfortunately the position which they had been given was in error by 45 seconds of arc, so that while they were carrying out their measurements, between January 14 and 18, they

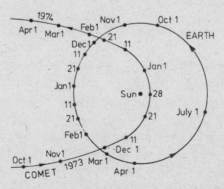

Fig. 15. Orbit of Kohoutek's Comet and positions of the earth, October 1973 to April 1974.

were pointing their equipment in the wrong direction. It is hardly surprising that their results were negative. One might even say that Kohoutek's Comet was obstinate to the last.

At least the comet's position was carefully and accurately measured. The orbit proved to be inclined at an angle of 14.3 degrees and to be highly elliptical. The estimated period is 75,000 years, and if this is approximately correct the aphelion distance is of the order of 320 billion miles, roughly 90 times the mean distance of Pluto.

So much, then, for Kohoutek's Comet, now back in the depths of space whence it came. West's Comet of 1976, our last bright visitor, was much more imposing—it too is nonperiodic, and on its outward journey it showed signs of disintegration. When we will see a more imposing visitor, we cannot tell. We can only hope that there will be more truly great comets in the near future than there have been in the recent past.

Donati's Comet of 1858. From an old woodcut.

The Great Comet of 1861 as seen with a 13-inch telescope on July 3. Drawing by W. de la Rue.

Coggia's Comet of 1874 as it appeared over the Pont-Neuf, Paris. From an old woodcut.

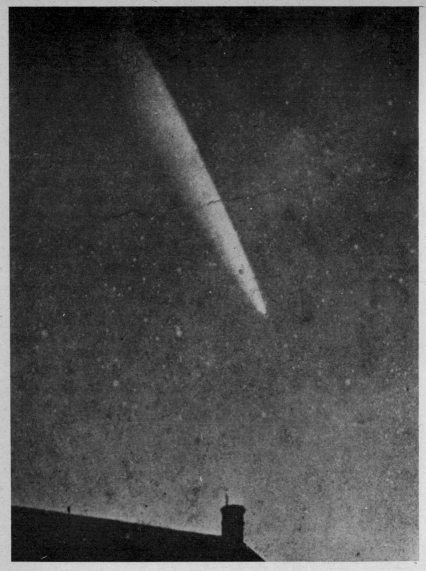

The Great Comet of 1882, from the Cape of Good Hope. Photograph by Sir David Gill. This was the first really good photograph of a comet, and so many stars were shown that Gill immediately saw the value of stellar photography.

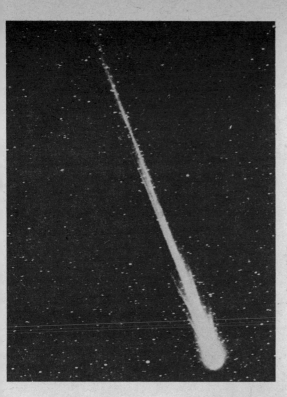

Comet Jurlov–Achmarov–Hassell, from Turku, Finland, April 21, 1939. Photograph by Väisälä and Oterma.

Comet Arend–Roland, from the Armagh Observatory, 1957. Photograph by E. M. Lindsay.

Mrkós Comet, from Greenwich Observatory, 1957. Photograph by E. A. Whitaker.

OPPOSITE: Comet Ikeya–Seki, November 1, 1965. Photograph by A. McClure.

Bennett's Comet of 1970 as seen from England on March 4. Photograph by
F. J. Acfield.

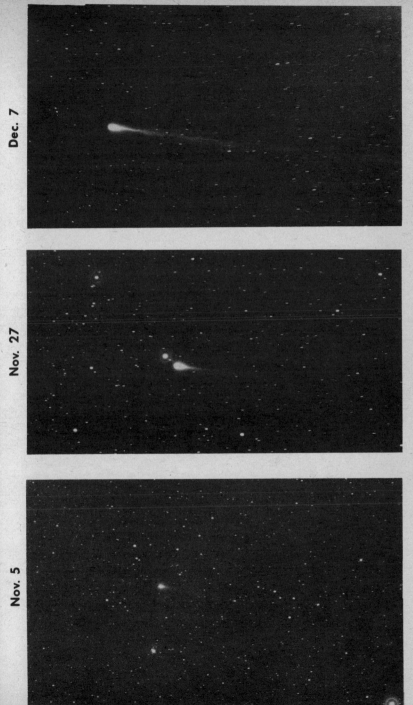

Nov. 5   Nov. 27   Dec. 7

Kohoutek's Comet, from Lowell Observatory, November 5 and 27 and December 7, 1973.

West's Comet, from Bulawayo, Rhodesia, March 30, 1976. Photograph by Jack McBain.

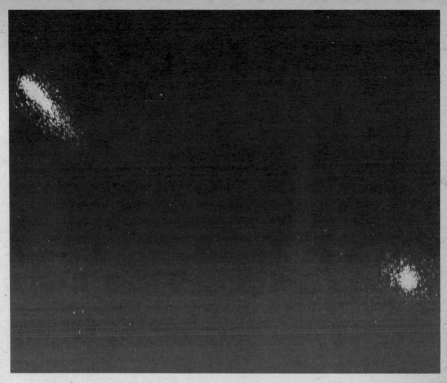

Biela's Comet, 1846. Drawing by Angelo Secchi.

The Leonid shower, 1833.
From an old woodcut.

Meteor Crater near Winslow, Arizona, 1964. Aerial photograph by Patrick Moore.

8 LOST COMETS

Most celestial bodies have very long lives. The earth and the moon have existed for at least 4,700 million years, and the sun is presumably even older; the planets move in stable orbits, and there is no reason to believe that any disaster will overtake them. Not so with the comets, which are fragile and ephemeral. On the cosmic scale they die quickly—and we have even seen one or two of them in their death throes.

A nonperiodic comet will be lost as soon as it moves out of the inner part of the solar system and will not be recovered. Thus we have lost all track of Donati, Arend–Roland, Bennett, Kohoutek, and many others; but there are no grounds for suggesting that they have broken up. Periodic comets may be lost either because their movements are not sufficiently well known or because of genuine disintegration.

If a short-period comet is not adequately observed over a period of at least several weeks, its orbit is bound to be uncertain, and the comet may not be found at subsequent returns. This has happened several times and is only to be expected. Then there are comets which have been violently disturbed by Jupiter or less frequently by some other planet, so that observers have been unable to locate them afterward. The classic instance of disturbance by Jupiter is that of Lexell's Comet.

This comet was discovered by Messier on June 14, 1770. It was visible with the naked eye, and its apparent diameter was five times as great as that of the full moon —not because it was exceptionally large, but because it was exceptionally near; it passed within 750,000 miles of the earth. The orbit was calculated by the St. Petersburg mathematician Anders Lexell, who gave it a period of 5.5 years. Unfortunately Lexell did not publish his results until 1778, by which time the whole situation had changed. He found that before 1767 the period had been much longer, but then an encounter with Jupiter had thrown the comet into the orbit which brought it close to Earth. Another approach to Jupiter in 1779 produced a further alteration, the net result being that the comet kept too far away from Earth to be seen at all. It has never been seen again, and we can hardly hope to recover it now.

A remarkable theory was presented in a book published in 1811—written originally by James Ferguson (1710–1774), who began his career as a Scottish shepherd boy and ended it as a famous writer on astronomy, and revised after Ferguson's death by the Scottish physicist Sir David Brewster (1781–1868). Brewster referred to the four asteroids which had been discovered between 1801 and 1808 and went on to say:

It is a very singular circumstance, that while two of the fragments, Juno and Vesta, are entirely free from any nebulous appearance, the other two fragments, Ceres and Pallas, are surrounded with a nebulosity of a most remarkable size. In the case of Ceres, this nebulosity is 675 English miles high; while the nebulosity of Pallas extends 468 miles from the body of the planet. It is obvious, that such immense atmospheres could not have been derived from the original planet, otherwise Juno and Vesta would also have been encircled with them; so that they must have been communicated to Ceres and Pallas, since the planet was burst. [Brewster was assuming, as many people still do today, that the asteroids were the debris of an old planet which disintegrated in the remote past.] Now, the Comet of 1770, if it is lost, must have been attracted by one of the planets whose orbit it crossed, and must have imparted to it its nebulous mass; but none of the old planets have received any addition to their atmosphere; consequently, it is highly probable that the Comet has passed near Ceres and Pallas, and imparted to them those immense atmospheres which distinguish them from all the other planets.

Fascinating indeed—but completely wrong. No planet could be endowed with an atmosphere in such a way, and in any case neither Ceres nor Pallas has any vestige of atmospheric mantle. Their escape velocities are far too low, and their images are as sharp and clearcut as those of all the other asteroids. Another interesting comment was made by the great French mathematician and astronomer Pierre Simon de Laplace (famous for his nebular hypothesis of the origin of the solar system). Laplace pointed out that if Lexell's Comet had been as massive as the earth, its effect during the encounter of 1770 would have been to shorten the length of our day by 2 hours and 47 minutes. The fact that nothing of the kind was observed made Laplace conclude that the mass of the comet was no more than 1/5000 that of the earth. Actually, the true value is very much less than this.

Lexell's Comet has vanished from our ken simply because it is now very faint and we do not know where to look for it; it has not disintegrated. But with other comets, the causes of "loss" are much more fundamental.

Consider Westphal's Comet, first detected in 1852 and described then as "pretty bright." It belonged to the so-called long-period class, with a revolution time of 61 years. It came back on schedule and was seen again in 1913, but it then faded out: apparently it did not survive its perihelion passage. There was no question of its having been pulled out of position into an unexpected orbit; it disintegrated and must now be regarded as defunct. In theory, it should have returned to perihelion on January 3, 1976, and searches were made for it just in case astronomers were wrong in "writing it off," but no trace of it was found. Brorsen's periodic comet, first seen in 1846, is another such casualty; and in 1926 Ensor's Comet became diffuse as it approached perihelion, and it too vanished as effectively as the hunter of the Snark.

Yet one must beware of jumping to conclusions. In 1892 British astronomer E. E. Holmes discovered a comet with a period of approximately 7 years; it was dimly visible with the naked eye and thus was one of the brightest of the short-period comets. At its subsequent returns it was fainter, and after 1906 it "went missing." It was listed as being extinct, but one energetic astronomer, Dr. Brian Marsden, was not satisfied. He made an exhaustive series of calculations, and as a result Holmes' Comet was found again at its return in 1964, although it had become very faint indeed. Its case is particularly instructive for that reason; the wastage of material at each perihelion passage is taking its toll.

Marsden was equally successful in tracking down another comet, Di Vico–Swift, which had not been seen since 1894, even though its period was a mere 6.3 years. This comet has also declined. In 1844, the year of its discovery by Di Vico, it was on the fringe of naked-eye visibility and had a short tail. It was badly placed at the next return, that of 1850, and nobody was surprised when it was missed. Yet it should have been well placed in late 1855, and when it could not be located, it was regarded as lost.

Then, in November 1894, Swift in California discovered a telescopic comet whose orbit was so like that of the lost Di Vico that there could be no serious doubt of its identity. Jupiter had been the culprit once more; a close approach to the giant planet in 1855 had caused a marked alteration into an orbit with a period of only 5.75 years. Yet another encounter, in 1897, twisted the orbit again—this time into a period of 6.4 years—and, not surprisingly, the comet was lost once more.

Nothing more happened until the 1960s, when Marsden took up the problem. His calculations proved to be amazingly accurate; and in the clear sky of his native Argentina in 1965, Dr. Arnold Klemola managed to photograph the comet, now called Di Vico–Swift, in just the place were Marsden had said it would be. The discovery was timely, because in 1968 a third encounter with Jupiter threw the comet back once more into a larger orbit. This means that it can never again become bright enough to be seen with the naked eye or even with binoculars.

We must, then, take all due precautions before mourning the death of a comet. But in the case of the most famous lost comet of all, Biela's, there can be no doubt whatsoever, and this brings up an important topic referred to earlier—the close association between comets and meteor streams.

In 1772 Charles Messier discovered a faint comet which seemed to be entirely unremarkable. It was also seen by another French observer, J. L. Montaigne, and was kept under observation for some time. In 1810 Friedrich Bessel, the German astronomer who was later to become famous as being the first man to measure the distance of a star, checked on the orbit of the 1772 comet and decided that it must be identical with a comet which had been seen in 1806. If it had a period of 6.75 years, it had returned several times in the interim without being detected.

Bessel predicted a return for 1826 and alerted his colleagues. One of these was an Austrian soldier, Captain Wilhelm von Biela, who was a skillful amateur astronomer. Von Biela managed to capture the comet; he saw it on February 27, 1826, and worked out that its period must be 6 years 9 months. Ten days later it was also seen by the French astronomer Adolphe Gambart and is sometimes referred to as Gambart's Comet, although Biela's sighting has priority.

The next return, in November 1832, was entirely normal. The perihelion passage of 1839 was missed because the comet remained too close to the sun, but there seemed no reason to doubt that Biela's Comet would be back once more in 1846, and in late 1845 it duly made its appearance. To everyone's surprise, it was not alone. It was accompanied by a second luminous patch, which developed into a second comet. The original object had split in two.

A detailed description was given in late January 1846 by Professor James Challis at Cambridge University, who was using the 12-inch Northumberland refractor. (Challis is today best remembered for not having discovered the planet Neptune, even though all the information was in his hands.) Challis said:

> There are certainly two comets. The north preceding is less bright and of less apparent diameter than the other, and has a minute stellar nucleus. . . . I think it can scarcely be doubted, from the above observations, that the two comets are not only apparently but really very near each other, and that they are physically connected. When I first saw the smaller, on 15 January, it was faint, and might easily have been overlooked. Now it is a very conspicuous object, and a telescope of moderate power will readily exhibit the most singular celestial phenomenon that has occurred for many years—a double comet.

Astronomers waited eagerly for the next return, that of 1852. This time the two comets were separated by over a million miles; they remained on view for several weeks.

In 1859 the position of the comet(s) was again so unfavorable that no observations could be expected, but conditions in 1866 should have been ideal, and searches began well ahead of time. They proved completely fruitless. Although the predicted position of the comet pair had been worked out with great accuracy,

Biela's Comet was conspicuous only by its absence.

Nobody had any real hope of finding the comet again at the next predicted return, that of 1872, but another line of investigation had opened. There had long been a suspicion that meteors might be related to comets, and that meteoritic material could well be spread out along the orbits of known comets; the Italian astronomer Giovanni Schiaparelli, best remembered now for his observations of the "canali" on Mars, had already found that the brilliant Perseid meteors moved in a path which was very like that of a known comet. Calculations by two German astronomers, H. L. D'Arrest and E. Weiss, showed that a meteor shower observable in late November each year could be associated with Biela's Comet and that there might be a major display in November 1872, at the time when the earth passed through the orbit of the missing comet.

The prediction was fulfilled. On November 27 a brilliant meteor shower was seen, and there can be no doubt that these meteors represented the debris of the dead comet. Since then the "Bieliid" shower has become much weaker, but a few meteors are still recorded as coming from the old source, so that even today we have not quite seen the last of Biela's Comet.

Why did Biela's Comet vanish so completely? There have been suggestions that the original division into two parts was caused by a close approach to Jupiter in 1842 and that the pull of the sun did the rest. But there is another episode which deserves to be put on record, even though it has never been fully explained. One astronomer who kept up his interest in the comet even after the fiasco of 1865 was Wilhelm Klinkerfues of Göttingen, and on November 30, 1872, he sent his English colleague, N. Pogson, at Madras in India, the cryptic message: "Biela touched Earth on 27th; search near Theta Centauri." (Theta Centauri is a bright southern-hemisphere star, never well seen from the United States and permanently below the horizon in Britain.) Pogson made a search, and on December 2 and 3, 1872, he actually observed a comet. Alas, bad weather and the approach of twilight conditions prevented him from seeing it again, and nothing more is known about it. However, Pogson was a highly experienced observer, and he described his comet as having a bright nucleus and an appreciable tail, so that there seems little room for error. On the other hand, it is inconceivable that the comet was Biela's; it must have been another, quite unconnected comet which merely happened to lie in the same region of the sky. After the lapse of more than a century, we can scarcely hope to solve the mystery now.

Another double comet was that of 1860, seen by the French astronomer E. Liais from Olinda in Brazil and always known as the Olinda Comet. Liais saw the two comets on February 27, the day after the discovery; he followed the pair until March, but on March 13 the secondary comet disappeared. Unfortunately nobody else saw the Olinda Comet at all, so that little more can be said about it; and some astronomers tend to doubt the authenticity of Liais's observations.

Some comet-meteor associations, however, are beyond doubt. One is the meteor shower connected with a 1973 comet, Giacobini–Zinner. The comet itself is not remarkable in appearance; it never becomes visible to the naked eye, although its orbit is well known, and it has been seen regularly since its original discovery by M. Giacobini from Italy in 1900. (It was missed in 1906, but in 1913 it was recovered by Zinner, a German—hence the double name.) In 1933 the earth made contact with the meteor swarm moving in the comet's orbit, and for about an hour or two meteors rained down—in some parts of Europe more than 15,000 were estimated to have been recorded within sixty minutes. A second shower of comparable intensity was seen in 1946, and this time astronomers were ready for it, so that it was well studied. Unfortunately, the swarm was subsequently perturbed by Jupiter, and we cannot be sure if or when there will again be a major display of "Giacobinids."

Well-known meteor showers also connected with comets include the Beta Taurids (June 24 to July 6 yearly) with Encke's Comet; the other Taurids (September 15 to December 15, with a maximum around November 14) also with Encke's; and both the Eta Aquariids (April 21 to May 12) and the Orionids (October 18 to 26) with Halley's, although this last association has been questioned lately. Then there are the Leonids of November 17, which are linked with the orbit of a faint periodic comet, Tempel 1 of 1866, which was lost for some time. The Leonids are not reliable. They used to produce major displays approximately every 33 years—in 1799, 1833, and 1866—but planetary perturbations interfered with the promised displays of 1899 and 1933. In 1966 the conditions seemed favorable. In England, I devoted a television program in my *Sky at*

Night series to the shower and asked enthusiasts to watch between midnight and dawn to record any meteors that might occur. We were disappointed; very few Leonids were seen, and one disgruntled viewer wrote: "Watched from midnight until 6 A.M. Meteors: from the sky—none. From the wife—plenty." In fact, the display occurred during daylight over Europe, so that we missed it by a few hours. From other parts of the world—Arizona, for example—it was magnificent, with a rate of more than 100,000 shooting stars per hour. The fact that the shower lasted for so short a time (only 4 hours) proved that the meteors are "bunched" rather than being spread more uniformly along the comet's orbit, as happens with the Perseids; rather ironically, our observations in the British Isles were more valuable scientifically than they would have been if we had seen the main display. Whether we will be treated to a further shower of celestial fireworks in 1999 depends upon whether the orbit is again shifted in the interim.

It would be an oversimplification to say that meteors are due to the breaking up of old comets, but of the association there can be no doubt. As I mentioned, the solid particles of a comet are of meteor size, which is why the "dust" in the tails can be pushed outward by the stream of low-energy particles coming from the sun.

What, then, about meteorites? Here there is no evidence of any cometary association; and, as noted, meteorites are much more nearly related to asteroids than to shooting stars. But it would be a pity not to mention the so-called Siberian Meteorite of 1908, because the evidence now indicates that the object was not really a meteorite at all.

The impact occurred on June 30, 1908, in the Tunguska region of Siberia. Apparently what was called a "fireball" appeared without warning and became as bright as the sun. Then came a violent shock, indicating that something massive had fallen. Mercifully, the whole region was uninhabited, and there were no casualties; if the object had landed upon a city the death toll would have been colossal. The local reindeer population suffered, and pine trees were blown down over an area more than 20 miles in diameter.

Because of the unsettled state of affairs in Russia, little information could be obtained at the time, and it was not until 1927 that an expedition went to investigate. It was led by the Russian astronomer L. A. Kulik, who had taken a special interest in the problem. It seemed likely that the impact had been caused by a meteorite, and there were, after all, cases of known meteorite craters—the most famous example being in Arizona, not far from the town of Winslow. The Arizona crater is almost a mile across, and many meteoritic fragments have been found in the area.

To his surprise, Kulik found no meteoritic material at all. There was plenty of evidence of devastation, but nothing in the form of solid debris from the sky. This was a puzzle and led to various remarkable theories; flying-saucer believers suggested that the "meteorite" was really a visiting space ship which had exploded on landing.

However, the results are understandable if we assume that the missile was a small comet. The ices making up the head of the comet would be evaporated by the heat generated on impact and would produce the shock wave that flattened the trees, while the comet gases would simply dissipate in the atmosphere. After a brief period all trace of the comet would be gone. Let me stress, once again, that cometary material is very insubstantial.

This theory would explain both the lack of cosmic debris and the absence of meteorite craters. There is no final proof, but it does seem very plausible. The Siberian case is the only likely cometary impact in recorded times, and it will probably remain in a class of its own for a long time to come. This is fortunate; although a comet could not destroy the earth, it could certainly wipe out a city. However, there is no danger of catastrophe when Halley's Comet comes back in 1986. It will not approach within millions of miles of the earth, so we will be well out of harm's way.

9 WHENCE COME THE COMETS?

A comet is a ghostlike thing. There is nothing ponderous about it, and, like a ghost, it can vanish without a trace. Where, then, does a comet originate?

This brings up the question of the origin of the solar system itself, about which there have been many theories. An early one, according to which the planets were pulled off the sun by the action of a passing star, has been investigated and found wanting. (Like many plausible-sounding theories, it is mathematically untenable.) It is overwhelmingly likely that the sun and the planets are condensations from an original cloud of dust and gas. It may be that the sun itself represents the central part of the cloud; it may be that the cloud once surrounded an already shining sun and the planets built up from the material over a long period of time. In any case, the earth's age is now considered to be around 4,700 million years, and the same is true of the moon, as is shown by analyses of the lunar samples brought back by the Apollo astronauts and the unmanned Russian probes.

No comet which makes regular returns to the sun can last for anything like so long as this. Therefore, either the shorter-period comets are of more recent origin, or they have spent so much of their lives in regions far from the sun that they have been able to avoid wasting away.

Today there are several main theories of cometary origin, so I shall deal with them one by one, saving the best until last.

The giant planet theory. Toward the end of the eighteenth century, the French mathematician Joseph Louis Lagrange suggested that comets might have been shot out of the giant planets. In those days Jupiter and Saturn were believed to be hot bodies, perhaps like miniature suns, and there seemed no reason to doubt that Uranus, discovered in 1781, had the same character. (Neptune, as noted, was not found until 1846.) This idea of miniature suns was not finally disproved until the 1920s. While it is true that the internal heat of a giant planet is considerable and in the case of Jupiter may attain half a million degrees, the outer gases are very cold. There is a fundamental difference between a star, which is self-luminous, and a giant planet, which is not.

About a hundred years ago the English astronomer R. A. Proctor worked out the ejection theory in detail. Basing his ideas on the fact that many of the short-period comets have their aphelia at roughly the distance of Jupiter's orbit, he concluded that the comets originated inside Jupiter itself. He regarded Jupiter's great red spot as a kind of supervolcano, puffing out comets regularly. Short-period comets which disintegrated would be steadily replaced by new ones.

Not many people agreed with Proctor, and little more was heard about the theory until 1953, when it was rather unexpectedly revived by the Russian astronomer S. K. Vsekhsviatskii of Kiev Observatory. One of the main objections has always been the great force needed to hurl the comet-making material away from Jupiter, where the escape velocity is 37 miles per second as against a mere 7 miles per second for Earth. When Vsekhsviatskii first put forward his hypothesis, he suggested that the "Jovian family" of short-period comets had been ejected from Jupiter and the longer-period comets from Saturn, Uranus, and Neptune respectively; later he amended the theory and proposed that comets could have been ejected from the four large Jovian satellites, Io, Europa, Ganymede, and Callisto. This sounds highly unlikely. Even Ganymede and Callisto, the largest of the four, are no more than comparable with the smallest planet, Mercury; Io is only slightly larger than our moon, and Europa is smaller. They do not appear to be active worlds, and any atmospheres around them are remarkably tenuous, as has been confirmed by the data sent back from Pioneer 10 in 1973 and Pioneer 11 in 1974. Moreover, there are serious mathematical objections to the whole concept of cometary material's being ejected from either a planet or a satellite, and modern astronomers as a whole are decidedly unimpressed.

The collection theory. This is my own term for the hypothesis first proposed by Lagrange's contemporary Laplace. Laplace believed that comets originated in an interstellar cloud which was captured by the sun. The modern version has been developed by R. A. Lyttleton, who, as previously noted, regards comets as flying gravel-banks.

In the collection theory, comets are produced when

the sun passes through an interstellar cloud, and there is a sort of "gravitational lens" effect, concentrating dust and frozen gases in the area opposite to the sun's motion through the cloud. Lyttleton reasons that the familiar comets must be recent acquisitions and cites the case of Halley's Comet, which loses a certain amount of mass every time it returns to perihelion. Reckoning backward, so to speak, it can be calculated that a mere 10 million years ago Halley's Comet would have been as massive as the earth if it had followed its present orbit ever since. This is clearly impossible, as Halley's Comet cannot have been suffering this steady wastage for anything nearly as long as 10 million years.

There is nothing implausible in the suggestion that the sun's latest encounter with a dust-and-gas cloud has been recent, but some mathematicians maintain that comets do not move in quite the way that they would be expected to do if they were produced as Lyttleton believes. One modification (not Lyttleton's) suggests that the collected material forms into a dust cloud, making a zone around the sun from which comets are built up.

Oort's Cloud. Immanuel Kant, the eighteenth-century German philosopher, had the germ of an idea when he wrote that comets are formed in remote regions and are made up of particles "of the lightest material there is." Suppose, then, that there is a "cloud" of comets moving around the sun at an immense distance—a sort of refrigerated cometary reservoir? This was proposed in 1930 by the Estonian astronomer Ernst Öpik and

worked out in more detail twenty years later in Holland
by the Dutch astronomer J. H. Oort.

According to Oort, comets are composed of the material left over after the formation of the main bodies of
the solar system. Normally they travel around the sun
in approximately circular paths, moving very slowly
(perhaps only an inch or two per second) and of course
quite beyond the range of our telescopes; in fact, what
has become known as Oort's Cloud may extend out
almost halfway to the nearest star. There may be upward of 100 million comets in the cloud, and most of
them remain in stable orbits. However, perturbations
by any passing star—or perhaps by collisions among the
comets themselves—could cause a change, putting the
affected comet into a path which would send it hurtling
toward the sun. At first the movement would be gradual, but as the distance lessened the velocity would
increase. When the comet approached the sun, it would
be moving at a tremendous rate; it would swing past
perihelion and return to the outer regions from which
it had come, unless it encountered a planet and was
forced into a short-period orbit.

This theory would explain many of the facts. It would
show why the short-period comets are faint; they are
losing some of their material at each return to perihelion, whereas the comets with very long periods (hundreds, thousands, or even millions of years) come back
so seldom that they have not wasted away. It would also
explain why bright comets tend to appear at intervals
of relatively few years, followed by a long interval during which no more are seen. The sun grazers of the
nineteenth century could well have been sent on their

way from the same part of Oort's Cloud as a result of the same perturbing influence. It has also been suggested that there may even be two clouds—one at about twice the distance of Neptune and the other much more remote, occupying the zone between 30,000 and 100,000 astronomical units from the sun. (The nearest known star, Proxima Centauri, is roughly 270,000 astronomical units away.) The middle of the main zone would therefore be about one light-year away from the earth.

Yet there are objections to this theory also, and some astronomers have no faith in a comet cloud of any description. First, how did the comets get there? If they were formed in what we may call the middle part of the solar system, where Jupiter now lies, they could have been hurled outward by Jupiter's gravitational perturbations and then forced into remote, near-circular orbits by the pulls of stars, but this involves some very special assumptions. Lyttleton has also stressed that there are simply not enough stars close enough to wrench numbers of comets away from the cloud and send them inward. Any normal stars lying within a few light-years of the earth would undoubtedly have been found long ago, and to suppose that there are quantities of "dead," nonluminous stars nearer than Proxima Centauri is straining the possibilities.

Obviously, ideas about the origin of comets are still in a state of flux. Cloud or no cloud? Gravel-banks or dirty ice ball—or something different from either? It would help immensely if an unmanned spacecraft could be sent to (or, better, through) a comet to see just what is to be found there. In fact, this is by no means

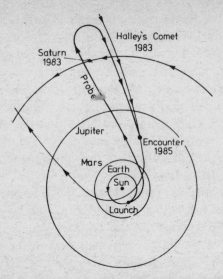

Fig. 16. Hypothetical space probe to Halley's Comet, making use of the gravitational pull of Saturn. The probe would be swung around Saturn in 1983 and would then move back toward the sun in a retrograde direction, catching up to the comet in 1985. It is not very likely that the experiment will be tried at the coming return of the comet because the launching would have to take place in the near future and no definite plans for this have been made.

an easy matter, even in this age of travel to the moon and rockets to the giant planets. The best hope is to contact a short-period comet whose orbit is not sharply tilted and which comes reasonably close to the earth; Finlay's Comet and D'Arrest's Comet have been suggested. Halley's Comet poses even greater problems, because of its retrograde motion. One suggested solution is to use the gravitational field of Saturn. If a probe were swung around Saturn in 1983, it could conceivably be hurled back into a retrograde orbit, so that it could "catch up" to its target even before Halley's Comet comes back into telescopic range. Whether or not this will be attempted remains to be seen, but it sounds much less farfetched today than reaching the moon did in, say, 1940.

I am well aware that this survey of cometary astronomy is very much an open-ended story. I hope, however, that I have managed to convey something of the subject's fascination and that my readers will take more than a passing interest the next time they see one of these strange, insubstantial visitors from outer space.

APPENDIX: TABLES
GLOSSARY
INDEX

TABLE I. Periodic Comets Observed at More Than One Return (Complete to 1975)

Comet	Period (Years)	Distance from sun (Astronomical units)		Eccentricity	Inclination	Number of appearances	Most recent return
		Perihelion	Aphelion				
Short-period comets							
Encke	3.3	0.34	4.09	0.85	12.0	50	1974
Grigg–Skjellerup	5.1	1.00	4.94	0.66	21.1	12	1972
Tempel 2	5.3	1.36	4.68	0.55	12.5	15	1972
Honda–Mrkós–Pajdušáková	5.3	0.58	5.49	0.58	13.1	5	1974
Neujmin 2	5.4	1.34	4.84	0.57	10.6	2	1927
Tempel 1	5.5	1.50	4.73	0.52	10.5	5	1972
Tuttle–Giacobini–Kresák	5.6	1.15	5.13	0.63	13.6	5	1973
Tempel–Swift	5.7	1.15	5.22	0.64	5.4	4	1908
Wirtanen	5.9	1.26	5.16	0.61	12.3	5	1974
D'Arrest	6.2	1.17	5.61	0.66	16.7	12	1970
Du Toit–Neujmin–Delporte	6.3	1.68	5.15	0.51	2.9	2	1970
Di Vico–Swift	6.3	1.62	5.21	0.52	3.6	3	1965
Pons–Winnecke	6.3	1.25	5.61	0.64	22.3	17	1970
Forbes	6.4	1.53	5.36	0.56	4.6	5	1974
Kopff	6.4	1.57	5.34	0.55	4.7	10	1970
Schwassmann–Wachmann 2	6.5	2.14	4.83	0.39	3.7	8	1974

TABLE I. (Cont.)

Giacobini–Zinner	6.5	0.99	5.98	0.71	31.7	9	1972
Wolf–Harrington	6.6	1.62	5.38	0.54	18.4	5	1971
Tsuchinshan 1	6.6	1.49	5.57	0.58	10.5	2	1971
Perrine–Mrkós	6.7	1.27	5.85	0.64	17.8	5	1968
Reinmuth 2	6.7	1.94	5.19	0.46	7.0	5	1974
Borrelly	6.8	1.32	5.84	0.63	30.2	9	1974
Johnson	6.8	2.20	4.96	0.39	13.9	4	1970
Tsuchinshan 2	6.8	1.78	5.40	0.51	6.7	2	1971
Harrington	6.8	1.58	5.60	0.56	8.7	2	1960
Gunn	6.8	2.45	4.74	0.32	10.4	—	—
Arend–Rigaux	6.8	1.44	5.76	0.60	17.8	4	1971
Brooks 2	6.9	1.84	5.39	0.49	5.6	11	1974
Finlay	6.9	1.10	6.19	0.70	3.6	9	1974
Holmes	7.0	2.16	5.20	0.41	19.2	5	1972
Daniel	7.1	1.66	5.72	0.55	20.1	5	1964
Harrington–Abell	7.2	1.77	5.68	0.52	16.8	3	1969
Shajn–Schaldach	7.3	2.23	5.28	0.41	6.2	1	1971
Faye	7.4	1.62	5.98	0.58	9.1	16	1969
Ashbrook–Jackson	7.4	2.29	5.33	0.40	12.5	4	1971
Whipple	7.5	2.48	5.16	0.35	10.2	6	1970
Reinmuth 1	7.6	2.00	5.76	0.49	8.3	6	1973
Arend	7.8	1.82	6.02	0.53	21.7	3	1967
Oterma	7.9	3.39	4.53	0.14	4.0	3	1958
Schaumasse	8.2	1.20	6.92	0.70	12.0	6	1960
Jackson–Neujmin	8.4	1.43	6.83	0.65	14.1	2	1970
Wolf	8.4	2.52	5.78	0.40	27.3	11	1967
Comas Solá	8.6	1.77	6.59	0.58	13.4	6	1969
Kwerns–Kwee	9.0	2.23	6.43	0.49	9.0	2	1972
Swift–Gehrels	9.2	1.35	7.44	0.69	9.3	2	1972

Name							
Neujmin 3	10.6	1.98	7.66	0.59	3.9	3	1972
Gale	11.0	1.18	8.70	0.76	11.7	2	1938
Väisälä 1	11.3	1.87	8.19	0.63	11.5	4	1971
Slaughter–Burnham	11.6	2.54	7.72	0.50	8.2	2	1970
van Biesbroeck	12.4	2.42	8.31	0.55	6.6	2	1966
Wild	13.3	1.98	9.24	0.65	19.9	2	1973
Tuttle	13.8	1.02	10.46	0.82	54.4	9	1967
Du Toit 1	15.0	1.29	10.85	0.79	18.7	2	1974
Schwassmann–Wachmann 1	15.0	5.45	6.73	0.11	9.7	—	—
Neujmin 1	17.9	1.54	12.16	0.78	15.0	4	1966
Medium-period comets							
Crommelin	27.9	0.74	17.65	0.92	28.9	4	1956
Tempel–Tuttle	32.9	0.98	19.56	0.90	162.7	4	1965
Stephan–Oterma	38.8	1.60	21.34	0.86	17.9	2	1942
Long-period comets							
Olbers	69.5	1.18	32.62	0.93	44.6	3	1956
Pons–Brooks	71.0	0.77	33.51	0.96	74.2	3	1954
Brorsen–Metcalf	71.9	0.49	34.11	0.97	19.2	2	1919
Halley	76.1	0.59	35.33	0.97	162.2	27	1910
Herschel–Rigollet	154.9	0.75	56.94	0.97	64.2	2	1939
Grigg–Mellish	164.3	0.90	59.14	0.97	109.8	2	1907
Lost periodic comets							
Brorsen	5.5	0.59	5.61	0.81	29.4	5	1879
Biela	6.6	0.86	6.19	0.76	12.6	6	1852
Westphal	61.9	1.25	30.03	0.92	40.9	2	1913

TABLE II. Periodic Comets Observed at Only One Return
(Complete to 1975)

Comet	Period (Years)	Year seen
Helfenzrieder	4.5	1766
Blanpain	5.1	1819
Du Toit 2	5.3	1945
Barnard 1	5.4	1884
Schwassmann–Wachmann 3	5.4	1930
Clark	5.5	1973
Brooks 1	5.6	1886
Lexell	5.6	1770
Kohoutek	5.7	1975
Pigott	5.9	1783
West–Kohoutek–Ikemura	6.1	1975
Kojima	6.2	1970
Taylor	6.4	1916
Spitaler	6.4	1890
Harrington–Wilson	6.4	1951
Barnard 3	6.5	1892
Churyumov–Gerasimenko	6.6	1969
Giacobini	6.6	1896
Schorr	6.7	1918
Swift	7.2	1895
Denning 2	7.4	1894
Metcalf	7.8	1906
Gehrels 2	7.9	1973
Denning 1	8.7	1881
Klemola	11.0	1965
Boethin	12.0	1975
Peters	13.4	1846
Gehrels 1	14.5	1973
van Houten	15.8	1961
Pons–Gambart	63.8	1827
Dubiago	67.0	1921
di Vico	75.7	1846
Väisälä 2	85.4	1942
Swift–Tuttle	120.0	1862
Barnard 2	145.4	1889
Mellish	145.3	1917

TABLE III. Notable Comets, 1680–1977

Date	Description	Discoverer
1680	Brilliant comet, visible in daylight	Gottfried Kirch
1744	De Chéseaux's six-tailed comet	Klinkenberg
1811	Largest recorded coma (1.25 million miles)	Honoré Flaugergues
1843	Brilliant daylight comet, superior to that of 1811. Longest recorded tail (200 million miles)	
1858	Donati's Comet; beautiful curved main tail	Giovanni Battista Donati
1861	Brilliant comet, Earth passed through tail	Jerome, Coggia, and Tebbutt
1862	Bright comet	Lewis Swift
1874	Coggia's Comet; bright naked-eye object	Coggia
1882	Brilliant daylight comet, well photographed by Sir David Gill	
1901	Bright southern comet of yellow hue	Paysandu
1910	Daylight Comet	
1927	Skjellurup's Comet (bright for a brief period)	Skjellerup
1947	Bright southern comet; brilliant for only a short while	
1948	Bright comet, seen first during a total solar eclipse	
1957	Arend–Roland; not particularly brilliant, but with interesting "spike" phenomenon	Arend and Roland
1957	Naked-eye comet (morning object, autumn) comparable with Arend–Roland	Mrkós
1962	Seki–Lines; bright	Seki and Lines
1965	Ikeya–Seki; brilliant from parts of the southern hemisphere	Ikeya and Seki

TABLE III. Notable Comets, 1680–1973

Date	Description	Discoverer
1969	Tago–Sato–Kosaka; bright, found to be surrounded by hydrogen cloud	Tago, Sato, and Kosaka
1970	Bennett's Comet; bright naked-eye object	Bennett
1973	Kohoutek's Comet; promised much more than it achieved	Kohoutek
1976	West's Comet; bright naked-eye object	West

GLOSSARY

The following glossary is chiefly confined to terms frequently used in this book.

Aphelion. The point farthest from the sun in the orbit of a body traveling around the sun. See *Perihelion.*

Asteroid, or *minor planet.* A very small planet, moving around the sun. Most asteroids keep to the part of the solar system between the paths of Mars and Jupiter, although some have orbits which bring them well away from the main swarm, and some may make close approaches to Earth.

Coma of a comet. The most prominent part of a comet—the "fuzz" surrounding the nucleus.

Comet. An object made up of small particles and tenuous gas, moving around the sun. Most comets travel in elliptical paths, although it is possible that the gravitational pulls of the planets may occasionally expel a comet from the solar system altogether.

Ellipse. A closed curve which may be described as a "stretched-out circle," although this description will offend mathematicians, or as an oval. The eccentricity of an ellipse depends upon how "long and thin" it is. If the eccentricity is zero, the ellipse has become a circle.

Escape velocity. The velocity a body needs to escape from the gravitational pull of a more massive body, assuming no further acceleration.

Galaxy. Any of various large, widely separated systems of stars, gas, and dust. The system of which the sun is a member (the Milky Way) contains approximately 100,000 million stars.

Head of a comet. The part which includes the nucleus and the coma.

Hyperbola. A very "open" curve. A comet thrown into an orbit of hyperbolic form would never return to the sun. However, no evidence of a comet moving in such an orbit has been found.

Ices. Frozen materials—not necessarily frozen water; it is possible to have "ammonia ice," and many "ices" are contained in comets.

Meteor. A small particle traveling around the sun. Meteors become visible as streaks of light when they enter the earth's atmosphere, because of friction against the air particles.

Meteorite. A larger body, which can reach the ground without being destroyed. Meteorites are not simply large meteors; they are more nearly related to asteroids.

Meteoroid. General term for meteoritic bodies in space.

Minor planet. See *Asteroid.*

Moon. Earth's only natural satellite. Also often, though rather inaccurately, applied to the satellites of other planets. See *Satellite.*

Nucleus of a comet. The most massive part, situated in the coma.

Orbit. The path of an astronomical body or manmade satellite around another body.

Parabola. An open curve. If a comet moves in a parabolic orbit, it will never come back to the sun.

Perihelion. The point nearest the sun in the orbit of a body traveling around the sun. See *Aphelion.*

Period of an astronomical body. The time taken by a planet or a comet to move once around the sun, or by a satellite to move once around its primary planet.

Periodic comet. A comet which returns to perihelion at regular intervals. Conventionally the term is restricted to comets with periods short enough for their returns to be predicted.

Perturbation. The disturbance produced by the gravitational pull of one astronomical body upon another. Thus, many comets have their orbits strongly disturbed by the influence of Jupiter, so that they are said to suffer "perturbations" by that planet.

Planet. A nonluminous body revolving around the sun and shining only by reflected sunlight. The nine principal planets are Mercury, Venus, Earth, Mars, Jupiter, Saturn, Uranus, Neptune, and Pluto.

Return of a comet. The time when a comet comes back to the inner part of the solar system. Halley's Comet takes 76 years to move once around the sun (its period), and we say that it "returns" every 76 years. The last return was in 1910; the next will be in 1986.

Satellite. A secondary body moving around a planet. (To be strictly accurate, the planet and the satellite move around the common center of gravity to their system.) Jupiter has 14 satellites, Saturn 10, Uranus 5, Neptune and Mars 2 each.

Solar system. The system which includes the sun, the nine principal planets, the satellites, asteroids, comets, and meteoroids.

Solar wind. Streams of low-energy, electrified particles sent out by the sun, constantly and in all directions. Apparently it is the solar wind which makes the tails of comets point more or less away from the sun.

Star. An intensely hot globe of gas, shining by its own light. The sun is a typical star; it lies at a distance of 93 million miles (1 astronomical unit, abbreviated A.U., from the earth.) The nearest of the so-called fixed stars (Proxima

Centauri) is over 24 million million miles, or 4.2 light-years away.

Tail of a comet. The part streaming out from the coma; it is made up of very small particles or very tenuous gas, or both, and always points roughly away from the sun. Not all comets have tails.

INDEX